Conversations at Work

PALGRAVE POCKET CONSULTANTS

Palgrave Pocket Consultants are concise, authoritative guides that provide actionable solutions to specific, high-level business problems that would otherwise drive you or your company to employ a consultant. Written for aspiring middle-to-senior managers working across business at any scale, they offer solutions to the most cutting-edge issues across modern business. Be your own expert and have the advice you need at your fingertips.

Available now:

ATTRACTING AND RETAINING TALENT
Tim Baker

MYTH-BUSTING CHINA'S NUMBERS
Matthew Crabbe

RISKY BUSINESS IN CHINA
Jeremy Gordon

THE NEW CHINESE TRAVELER
Gary Bowerman

THE WORKPLACE COMMUNITY
Ian Gee and Matthew Hanwell

PEOPLE DATA
Tine Huus

PUBLIC RELATIONS IN CHINA
David Wolf

MAKING SOCIAL TECHNOLOGIES WORK
Ronan Gruenbaum

Forthcoming titles:

MANAGING ONLINE REPUTATION
Charlie Pownall

CRISIS MANAGEMENT
Alex Singleton

CREATING A RESILIENT WORKFORCE
Ivan Robertson and Cary Cooper

Series ISBN 9781137396792

About the authors

Dr Tim Baker is a thought leader, international consultant and successful author (www.winnersatwork.com.au). Tim was recently voted as one of *The 50 Most Talented Global Training & Development Leaders* by the World HRD Congress, which is awarded by a distinguished international panel for professionals "who are doing extraordinary work" in the field of HRD. He is the author of *The 8 Values of Highly Productive Companies: Creating Wealth from a New Employment Relationship* (Australian Academic Press, 2009), *The End of the Performance Review: A New Approach to Appraising Employee Performance* (Palgrave Macmillan), and *Attracting and Retaining Talent: Becoming an Employer of Choice* (Palgrave Macmillan). Tim has conducted over 2430 seminars, workshops and keynote addresses to over 45,000 people in 11 countries across 21 industry groups and regularly writes for HR industry press. Tim can be contacted at tim@winnersatwork.com.au.

Aubrey Warren is an experienced communication and leadership trainer, lecturer, coach, and writer who has contributed to the professional development of thousands of people across Australia and internationally since 2001. With a background in media production, Aubrey has published *The Situational Leader* e-newsletter since 2007. He is Australia's Situational Leadership® master trainer for the Center for Leadership Studies in the US and teaches communication and leadership for the QUT Graduate School of Business and its executive development programs.

Promoting a Culture of Conversation in the Changing Workplace

Conversations at Work

Tim Baker
WINNERS-AT-WORK Pty Ltd, Australia

Aubrey Warren
Managing Director, Pacific Training and Development, Australia

First published 2015 by
PALGRAVE MACMILLAN

Palgrave Macmillan in the UK is an imprint of Macmillan Publishers Limited, registered in England, company number 785998, of Houndmills, Basingstoke, Hampshire RG21 6XS.

Palgrave Macmillan in the US is a division of St Martin's Press LLC, 175 Fifth Avenue, New York, NY 10010.

Palgrave Macmillan is the global academic imprint of the above companies and has companies and representatives throughout the world.

Palgrave® and Macmillan® are registered trademarks in the United States, the United Kingdom, Europe and other countries.

ISBN 978–1–137–53416–3

This book is printed on paper suitable for recycling and made from fully managed and sustained forest sources. Logging, pulping and manufacturing processes are expected to conform to the environmental regulations of the country of origin.

A catalogue record for this book is available from the British Library.

A catalog record for this book is available from the Library of Congress.

Typeset by MPS Limited, Chennai, India.

Contents

List of Figures and Tables

Figures

Tables

Introduction

Organizational life is increasingly complex. Globalization, technology, disruption, and constant change affect public and private organizations, the large and the small, the contemporary and the traditional. But there's one apparently simple thing that they all share and that is both part of the increasing complexity they face and also a key to managing that complexity.

Organizations are conversations. At its heart, the life of any organization exists in, and is sustained through, the conversations that are taking place inside, around, and about it. Organizations are groups of people interacting with each other to achieve outcomes. The interactions that enable people to work together and produce are experienced through dialogue and conversation, both direct and indirect, and using a variety of means and formats. These conversations – formal and informal, simple and detailed, short and long – shape and reflect the culture of organizations and the teams and groups within them. Our conversations become our experience of our relationships and our work.

Conversations at Work is for managers, HR professionals, consultants, and everyone who is interested in changing the culture of their organization through improved dialogue. We are interested in assisting leaders to elevate employee engagement, learning, performance, innovation, quality, and problem-solving through better conversations.

Since Peter Senge's seminal work on the learning organization,[1] organizations have continued to struggle with the challenge of creating a culture of learning, innovation, and engagement. We believe the focus needs to be on the quality of dialogue between people and on having the right conversations at work. Essentially, this book is about getting back to a basic building block of human interaction and productive organizational life: the conversation.

Organizations are a series of conversations. But it is the quality of these conversations that matters and it's the quality of conversations that we are interested in. There are many barriers and roadblocks to developing a conversation culture. These barriers and roadblocks will be discussed in Part I; some practical strategies are offered as a means of changing the culture of organizations. Creating a culture of conversation is not as easy as it sounds. It is not just a matter of teaching managers to actively listen. It is a psychological change that is needed; changing the thinking – the mindset – of leaders is more important than developing a new skills-set.

In Part II, we look at the different conversations people have at work. There are conversations to build relationships; conversations to develop people; conversations to make decisions; and conversations to take and review action.

Part III looks at the skills required to have quality conversations.

Good quality conversation is sadly neglected in our society. It's not that we don't share information or talk to each other – indeed we're increasingly overloaded with information and bombarded by incoming messages via text, email, and social media. But little of that qualifies as good quality conversation; too often it's simply a transactional exchange of data. And while that's necessary and unavoidable, it's not conversation.

Some people think we must be possessed with some special God-given skill to have successful conversations – how often do we hear the phrase "the art of conversation," as if there is an innate talent excluding most of us. Although there are undoubtedly some instinctive personality traits that make conversation easier for some than others, there are also practical skills that can be learned by anyone willing to develop themselves.

The culture of conversation

Are we having less conversations now than previously, or are the conversations just different? There has been a growing trend for managers to learn the skills of having conversations, particularly difficult conversations. Imagine for a moment if you told your grandparents that you were having training to learn to have conversations at work. They would undoubtedly be amused. Conversations are still occurring, in the lunchroom, at the water cooler, in the car park, even in the bathroom! So why are we being challenged with conversations in the workplace? Or was it always a challenge, and it is only now that we are recognizing the importance and value of quality conversations?

Have we lost the need for face-to-face conversation in our technologically-driven world? It used to be that instead of talking face-to-face with people, we would call them on the telephone. Then we faxed them. Then we emailed them. Now we text them or "connect" with people through social media. In the midst of all of this rapid "communication," conversing one-on-one with people seems to be an old-fashioned thing to do. It is much quicker and easier to press a few buttons. While face-to-face conversations are undoubtedly the richest and usually most effective form of human communication, there's an illusion of convenience and connectivity through technology that can rob us of the quality that face-to-face conversation can offer. The question every contemporary manager must address is: How often am I using (or even hiding behind) technology when a face-to-face conversation is possible, or preferable?

Of course, while most of us would agree that the most powerful way to understand and influence others is through face-to-face communication in the same room, that option is not always possible. Increasingly, we are conversing with people in other cities or countries. Technology is undeniably a vital substitute. But we also know from our work in organizations that there is an over-reliance on the use of technology when face-to-face conversations can be arranged.

Both of us think communication technology is an essential resource for managing and we believe it should be used to its maximum potential. But it has its limitations. Technology seems to offer convenience, especially when the organizational context presents barriers to real, real-time conversations. It is these opportunities that are being lost – and sometimes being prevented – in contemporary organizational life.

When challenged about this, some managers will then say to us: "I don't have time for conversations. I have too much real work to do. I have too many emails that need answering and meetings to attend." Which makes us wonder what a manager's "real work" is!

Organizations reflect the people in them. And people reflect their culture. So we shouldn't be surprised to find this paradox of an over-communicated, always-connected society neglecting something as basic as the richness and power of conversations. If you commute to work on public transport, take a close look at the people on the bus or train this evening on the way home. We'll bet 90 per cent of them will have their heads down, staring at a screen of some kind. When these people get home they will be transfixed by at least one other screen, the TV, in-between tweets and Facebook updates. In the midst of our technology-mediated communication, we may be losing sight of the value and importance of conventional conversation.

Like many other authors, we strongly believe in the need to train managers how to have effective conversations with their staff. The conversations that people avoid most are the tough conversations. And yet these are the conversations they ought to be engaging in. More often than not, difficult conversations go better than anticipated. Managers carry around this fear in their head that the other person will react irrationally. Consequently, they avoid the anticipated confrontation and may send them an email instead. Their rationalization may be that we need to document the poor performance for legal reasons. But the real issue is fear of face-to-face conversation about tough issues. Even though those same managers will typically say that if there was an issue that needed to be brought to their own attention they would definitely want their manager to discuss it personally with them. And it's not just managers who say this. We all like to think we can deal with these things in adult, accountable ways by talking them through.

Another typical way of avoiding a face-to-face encounter about a tough issue is for the manager to make a statement reinforcing appropriate standards at the next staff meeting, hoping the person it is aimed at gets the message. Good luck with that!

Conversations at Work is pitched at the practicing manager. In addition to our extensive experience with client organizations, we have scanned the literature on conversations. At one end of the spectrum, the material available on conversations is often too esoteric and theoretical to be of much practical use. At the other end of the spectrum, there is a plethora of books that are too basic and simply reiterate "Communication 101." We therefore felt that there was a need to offer what is hopefully a thought-provoking and insightful book, to advance the quality of the conversation in the organizations you are working in by harnessing the research, theories, and models of effective communication and presenting this in practical, everyday workplace terms. We hope, and believe, that *Conversations at Work* will challenge, stretch, and develop your communication skills and, in the process, enable you to improve the quality of your team and organization – one conversation at a time.

Enjoy.

chapter 1

Organizations are Conversations

In the grand scheme of things, our lives are a network of conversations about a host of topics with a variety of people in an array of contexts.

One of the authors remembers vividly a situation where two civil engineers working on a complex project were not too civil with each other. They sat in an office cubicle, facing each other. The only thing separating them was a partition. One of the engineers was quite upset with the other over some details that were overlooked in the large-scale project they were working on together. He reacted to this situation by firing off an angry email to his colleague sitting a meter away. His email contained words such as "unprofessional" and "careless." He did this when he could have simply got out of his chair and had a conversation with his colleague – sharing his concerns about the overlooked details in the construction project and discussing solutions. The other engineer, understandably very angry and defensive about this email, fired off a heated email response with his own accusations and also copied in the project manager! Not a verbal word was uttered. In isolation this seems like a ludicrous situation, but unfortunately it happens too often in organizations.

Managers in all industries the world over are reluctant to sit down with their charges and converse on important matters beyond essential task-specific activities and projects. A typical example of this occurs when a manager is faced with substandard performance by a team member. The manager rationalizes that it would "open a can of worms" if they confronted the team member face-to-face about the issue, so they leave it for the annual or semi-annual performance review. By the time the performance review rolls around, the poor-quality work may have caused other negative consequences, and surely resulted in additional frustration for the manager. Combined with other performance problems, by the time the performance review occurs, there is undoubtedly a long list of poor performance misdemeanors that need confronting. Needless to say, this doesn't make for a very positive conversation for either the manager or team member. When these misbehaviors are finally broached, sometimes several months later, it raises the understandable question in the mind of the team member: "Why didn't you talk to me about it when the incident or incidents occurred?" We can all recall examples from our past experience when timely conversations could and should have occurred, but didn't. Sadly, the scenarios described in this chapter are not uncommon incidents in the workplace and they highlight the conversation deficit that exists in many organizations.

In a culture that avoids dealing with problems when they happen, the positive conversations also get neglected. For instance, how often do managers initiate conversations with their team members about their strengths and innate talents and how they can be better utilized in their current and future roles? Not nearly enough, if at all. Not at all, is what most people tell us. Working relationships suffer because of this or, at the very least, are not enhanced.

Conversations are omnipotent

The health of the working relationship between people, particularly manager and employee, mostly depends on the quality and frequency of their interactions. We are referring specifically here to the conversations they engage in, or don't engage in. Relationships grow and develop as a consequence of worthy conversations. Relationships also wither and decline as a consequence of poor or infrequent conversations. To illustrate the point, when we meet someone for the first time, our conversations are harmless and shallow. We converse in a "safe" zone, not wanting to reveal too much of ourselves or offend the other person. As we get to know the other person through sharing experiences, trust builds and we are more inclined to reveal more of ourselves, and our conversations become richer and more in-depth. As we feel safer, we risk more in the conversation and the relationship broadens and deepens. Conversely, when we grow apart from someone and become remote and distant, our conversations become less frequent and more superficial, just like when we first met. Conversations are indeed the drivers for better relationships, personally and professionally, and are also barometers of those relationships.

With the aid of technology, organizational and personal conversations occur in an increasingly wider array of forms and contexts. Despite this, and despite our need for deeper and more thoughtful conversations to cope with the increasing complexity we have to deal with, the kinds of conversations we have in the workplace have not altered much. The vast majority of organizational conversations are still task-specific.

The vast majority of organizational conversations are still task-specific.

Although based on the task-at-hand, conversations via any medium continue to be formal or informal, short or long, direct or indirect. Formal conversations are usually set pieces scheduled for a particular time and place, conducted either in person or through real-time technology. Informal conversations include the countless impromptu and incidental encounters that take place daily in every workplace. These informal conversations can be underestimated and often carry far greater potential for influence than formal communication.

With the evolution of the boundaryless organization, we are engaging in conversations with an increasingly wider range of stakeholders. Again, these multifarious conversations – whether face-to-face or not – are formal or informal, short or long, direct or indirect. And while most of these conversations are also task-specific, each conversation also feeds into individual and collective narratives that go well beyond the specific task. They also shape our opinions and understanding of people, relationships, projects, and issues.

Boundaryless organizational life also means that CEOs who may once have been distant figures to many of their staff, authority figures who occasionally made broad pronouncements, now are expected to engage in regular conversations with the entire organization. These human interactions occur in person, face-to-face, or virtually, increasingly, through social media. In any case, the expectations for more interaction are real and necessary – whether you're a CEO or local team leader, and whether your conversations are face-to-face or enabled by technology.

A T   T H E   C O A L   F A C E   ...

Conversing with a virtual team

Megan leads a global team of 60 people. She's based at a home office in Australia and has to manage across a wide range of cultures, projects, and time zones. For her, a key is maintaining the connection she has with each team member.

"One thing I feel passionately about is that technology enables me to work virtually, but it's about the people," she explains. "Whether it's a traditional bricks and mortar team or a virtual team, my job as a leader is to make sure that people are looked after."

Megan has also learned that with virtual teams you have to actively create opportunities for conversations. "The biggest difference from working in a traditional face-to-face team structure is that you have to create opportunities for people to come together rather than just expect that they'll come naturally," she says. "When you're working in a virtual team everything you do needs to be more conscious and overt because you need to make sure that you create a structure for the team to come together and be grounded in the same purpose. As a leader, that's your responsibility."

In addition to the conversations we have with others, we also engage in constant conversations with ourselves, sometimes consciously and other times subconsciously. While we don't focus on these conversations in *Conversations at Work*, they influence – and are influenced by – the many other conversations we are a part of. Internal dialogue profoundly reflects and reshapes the mental models we use in communicating, interpreting, interacting, and making decisions.

In the grand scheme of things, our entire lives are a network of conversations about a host of topics with a variety of people in a range of contexts. And that is something to celebrate and manage every day – one conversation at a time.

The manager as conversationalist

Have you ever considered how much time of your day is devoted to communication of some description? Without a shadow of a doubt, the vast majority of a manager's work is communicating to others in some shape or form. Gregory Bateson, a well-known anthropologist, goes so far as to suggest that, "everything a leader does is communicative as it sends a message both about the content and the relationship."[1] And probably the most common and important vehicle for communication is conversation. Some conversations are planned, some spontaneous. Some conversations initiate activity and others are a result of activity. Some are pleasant while some are tough. Some conversations are long, some are short, sharp and to the point. Some conversations are informal, while others are quite formal. Some occur in the office and others in the field, some in the board room and others in the coffee shop. Some are useful and others not so. Some help the situation, while others hinder the situation. Some conversations are simple and others are complex. The combinations and permutations of conversations are endless. And their presence is constant.

Managing the ebb and flow of conversations is a core skill of leadership. Although, strangely, it is not explicitly taught in business schools. It is only within the last few years that leadership conversations have become a topic of conversation in the management literature.

Conversations are the currency of human interaction. Organizational conversations cover a vast array of people. There are conversations with customers, conversations with stakeholders, conversations with suppliers, conversations with managers and employees; millions of conversations. The types of conversations vary too. There are developmental conversations, relationship building conversations, action-orientated conversations, decision-making conversations, friendly conversations, unfriendly conversations, hard conversations, soft conversations, pointless conversations, focused conversations. Conversations are omnipotent.

Despite the ubiquitous presence of conversations at work, the research indicates that both executives and more junior leaders are less than proficient at many elements of what might be considered essential engagement and communication skills. This is a finding from thousands of leaders who have been evaluated through DDI's assessment centers.[2] The research showed that leaders are not effective at clarifying situations before acting on them, which suggests they are not conversing with key people in the organization. In fact, 90 per cent of leaders rely on their own ideas rather than seeking involvement from their team, and 89 per cent were deficient in listening and responding to interpersonal cues from others. Further, there is a lack of clarity around decision-making and, disturbingly, only 5 per cent of the leaders sampled are effective in building trust in their interactions with team members.

This study is consistent with previous global research from DDI that found 60 per cent of employees felt their manager had damaged their self-esteem at some point. It gets worse. Employees would rather suffer a bad hangover, do housework, or see their credit card bill than face the prospect of sitting through a performance discussion with their boss. One in three respondents indicated that they never or only sometimes consider their manager to be effective, and 37 per cent say they are only sometimes or never motivated to give their best by their leader. On the other hand, these employees surveyed indicated that if they had the opportunity to work for their "best ever" leader, they could be 20 to 60 per cent more productive.[3] This is consistent with our observations. Scary stuff indeed!

Developing a conversation culture

According to Dik Veenman and Graham Hart of *The Right Conversation*, a UK-based consultancy,[4] organizations that thrive on dialogue typically have two underpinning aspects: a conducive climate and the right skills. "Climate" here refers to the culture and environment of the organization and the removal of barriers to having authentic conversations. This may include an absence of both physical and psychological obstacles. "Skills" refers to the ability to conduct and engage in good conversation. The barrier, in other words, is the manager's lack of capacity to conduct meaningful conversations. Veenman and Hart argue that without attention to both dimensions – climate and skills – a culture of conversation is unlikely to be sustainable. We cover both of these dimensions throughout the book. Promoting the right conversations at work is the intersection between climate and skills. There are a range of factors we cover within each dimension that either encourage or detract from dialogue in organizations.

James Kouzes and Barry Posner, in their book: *Credibility: How Leaders Gain and Lose It, Why People Demand It*, state that "leadership is a relationship."[5] We wholeheartedly agree. But it raises the question: "How are these relationships developed?" Leadership is expressed and relationships developed through meaningful dialogue with team members on a range of matters over time. Conversations are the vehicle for building strong, vibrant, professional working relationships. If organizations are conversations, then great conversations are the foundations of flourishing organizations.

But many managers are overworked. They tell us they have no time for conversations. Beyond the standard conversations we all engage in, meaningful conversations are usually not considered a high priority. "Once we get our work done we can have conversations" is the common refrain. But we think having profound conversations at work is the essence of leadership; it is the *work* of leadership.

And it is not just about priorities. It's also about culture and mindset. The command and control mindset of management is still alive and well in most organizations we come across. This top-down management paradigm is an inhibiting factor too. The authoritarian model of leadership is reliant on hierarchy and promotes a downward channel of communication. The information that filters down in hierarchical organizations is typically one-way, with the unequal power dynamic discouraging genuine dialogue. Yet, as Lynda Gratton and Sumantra Ghoshal remind us:

> Conversations lie at the heart of managerial work. It is (how managers) teach and inspire, motivate and provide feedback, plan and take decisions.[6]

Conversation is more than simply communicating instructions or indulging in idle chatter.

We are not necessarily referring to the idea of just having efficient transactional conversations either. Jim McCann, the CEO of *1-800-Flowers.com*, in his book, *Talk is (Not) Cheap*, talks about conversing with intimacy, not efficiency. He says:

> If you're watching the clock, you're not conversing. Speed encourages an efficient exchange of information, but unhurried conversation is what creates a bond and reveals a truth.[7]

Neither are we suggesting that managers ought to sit around all day and have long, drawn-out conversations with all and sundry. But far too often we assume in business that the bottom-line is the driver of all interactions. Everyone wants to make money, it's true. But everyone *needs* interaction and connection to sustain the money-making process and to ensure new opportunities are identified, shared, and developed.

Pivotal leadership

Richard Bowman, in his paper, "The Real Work of Department Chair," observes that managers do not manage departments or even functions; they manage conversational inquiry that engages others in creating possibilities, breakthroughs, and a sustainable future for their common enterprise.[8] Pivoting from one conversation to another is the essence of modern management. "Pivotal leadership" is a term coined by Kevin Barge in his reflections on leading.[9] Barge reflects on his own leadership and how he needed to maintain his flexibility to move swiftly from one conversation to another. Pivotal leadership characterizes the complexity of coordinating the balance of being involved in multiple conversations about a range of matters and trying to make sense of these in shaping a constructive outcome.

More specifically, there are two important aspects to pivotal leadership. The first ability is to move from one conversation to the next rapidly within the context of organizational demands. Second, pivotal leadership means balancing the needs of being in the here and now, giving complete focus to the other person in the conversation, and simultaneously considering the periphery of activity surrounding the leader. Communication for a leader is dealing with the complex assortment of tasks, activities, deadlines, and personalities. To be able to make sharp turns at critical points in the flow of myriad conversations, and encourage others to do the same, is the challenge.

There are several drivers that suggest that conversational leadership is now coming to the fore. We know that leadership is transitioning from a command and control paradigm to a collaborative affair, albeit too slowly for our liking. Since people are the organization's competitive advantage, innovation and continuous improvement is the province of everybody and not just the leader. To elicit, stimulate, create, and evaluate ideas, leaders have to engage teams and individuals in this process. The connectivity of the world of work and the individual participants means that hierarchy must now give way to cross-functional organizational communication. People can now have access to and talk with anyone from the CEO to the janitor, and everyone in-between. The potential for conversations is greater and exposure is increasing.

Two interesting movements are now evolving that exemplify this new age of connectivity and access and the demand this creates for genuine conversations: crowd sourcing and moving from the complex to the simple in human resource management.

A T T H E S C R E E N F A C E ...

The emerging employee conversation

Social media is undeniably changing the way in which employees' voices are heard. Addressing the role of "social media and employee voice," CIPD, a UK-based HR and people development association, published a report in 2013. In it, they noted that:

"In recent years, as a result of the relentless advance of social media, employee voice is evolving rapidly. The greatest difference is the shifting patterns of communication, from being one-way or two-way to being multi-directional. This has moved voice on from giving employees a say behind closed doors to enabling them to engage in an open forum. It is hard to ignore and as such is voice with muscle.

"For the first time, social technologies are allowing new forms of collaboration that comprise mechanisms for making collective decisions. This aggregation is crucial in the evolution of employee voice because it is a necessary condition under which the wisdom of crowds can be harnessed. The result is a new form of collective employee voice that is mobile, organised and intelligent."[10]

The wisdom of the crowds makes sense in times of accelerated change and uncertainty. And with technology delivering the capacity to reach everyone, quality conversations become essential to facilitating collective insight. Quality conversations are likewise at the heart of improving our management of people. We have managed over the last two decades to progressively overcomplicate this work. We sense there is a yearning to get back to basics; to understand that fundamentally we are dealing with people, not "human resources," or even "human capital." There is a thirst for a humanization of the workplace. Organizations want and need engaged workers and respectful, ethical, and accountable managers. These mutual needs can only really be fostered and nurtured through conversational leadership.

Conversation synchronicity

Conversation-based leadership may sound easy, but it's not. It's a skill, and developing it takes effort. Kevin Barge talks about the interesting concept of "synch your conversation." In his words, "I became fascinated with the pacing, rhythm, and mesh of tasks and conversations and what needed to be in place for tasks and conversations to move forward."[11] Juggling these capabilities is what he refers to as synching conversations. In other words, synching conversations is about the coordination of a host of inevitable conversations leaders have, or need to have, each with their unique tempo and speed.

How can leaders manage the accomplishment of important tasks on the one hand and give team members sufficient autonomy and space to enable them to be enterprising on the other? How do leaders balance the inevitable reporting processes that are required and at the same time not overburden team members with administration? How can a leader keep certain projects moving at a rapid pace and at the same time give team members the room to achieve their tasks and responsibilities? All of these dilemmas require a certain synchronicity.

There are a growing number of scholars who predict the end of the job and others that predict the end of the corporation. But while jobs as we know them may well disappear or, at the very least, be reshaped, work itself will not disappear. Similarly, while corporations may also become obsolete, or at least continue to morph and change, organizations of people working together towards a common goal will undoubtedly continue in some shape or form. And so working relationships between individuals and organizations of people will continue, albeit in different and more complex manifestations. This implies that conversation leadership and the ability to juggle its complexity is here to stay as a dominant feature of the world of work.

These human interactions and working relationships will continue to need nourishment. Conversations will have an enduring role to play. As the relationship between employer and employee continues to be less formal and more flexible, conversations will become an even more important lynchpin of the employment relationship. As power shifts from positional authority to personal influence, managers will need to engage in more eclectic conversations and dialogue with employees, and with an expanding array of stakeholders.

Benefits of conversations

Due to their frequency and importance, we believe there are economic, social, and psychological benefits in having better conversations at work. Our hypothesis is that by improving the quality (and frequency) of our conversations, managers have a practical, cost-effective, readily available communication vehicle to elevate the performance and well-being of organizational members, teams, enterprises, and, ultimately, society-at-large.

After all, it is the quality of conversations that determines everything in organizations: employee turnover, levels of engagement, innovation and continuous improvement, growth and development, understanding and appreciation, and productivity and profitability.[12] Yet, we witness a dereliction of meaningful conversations in the name of busyness. And this neglect of conversing erodes both the confidence and skills of leaders to engage in having proper conversations, and the confidence and respect of those they are trying to lead. It is a Catch-22.

This book is ultimately about promoting constructive dialogue in organizations. We believe, for all the reasons we have stated, that meaningful conversations are the lifeblood of organizations. By this, we are referring to constructive conversations between executives, managers, and frontline staff, one-on-one, in meetings, online, and by phone. Research conducted by The Right Conversation, the UK-based consultancy, supports our hypothesis. Their research illustrated the following:

- Overwhelmingly there is a positive correlation between the quality of the conversation and organizational effectiveness.
- More specifically, the quality of conversations has a direct impact on employee engagement, relationships with key stake-holders, and the strategic development of the organization.
- There are two dimensions that are important in improving dia-logue: creating the right environment and the mindset and skills of leaders.
- Although there is widespread recognition of the value and importance of conversations, only a relatively small number of organizations are investing in skill development.

• All organizations indicated that there was scope for improvement in organizational dialogue.[13]

We both teach in the MBA program at the Queensland University
of Technology. If you have completed an MBA, you are aware that
it is a demanding program, covering an extensive range of concepts
and a huge amount of information. It is interesting to speculate on
the question: "If we only had 30 minutes, what would we teach
our MBA students?" We have had a conversation about this. Our
response was immediate and straightforward. We would emphasize
the power and importance of good conversations because
those conversations hold the potential to unlock and unleash
the knowledge and resources needed to achieve business goals.
These conversations would cover customers and clients, between
employees, with stakeholders, between managers, with managers.
The list is endless. Further, we would point out the need for leaders
to think differently about their work; to appreciate the significance
and value of conversations and organizational dialogue as a critical
component of leadership.

As the traditional employment relationship disintegrates and
becomes a thing of the past, and a new employment relationship
blossoms, we think this provides fertile ground for promoting
quality conversation. Before our eyes, the employment relationship
or psychological contract is dramatically changing between the
individual and organization, characterized by management and
labor. Organizations are reflecting the dramatic changes in society.
Traditional power relationships are breaking down, a desire for
engagement is on the rise. Capitalizing on the wisdom, intelligence,
and know-how of people is now the difference between an average-
performing organization and the successful enterprise.

We have tried to convey the message here in Chapter 1 that organizations are indeed an ongoing series of all sorts of conversations. They

happen everywhere, at anytime, with anyone; they are pervasive. Improving the dialogue in organizations is our primary focus in *Conversations at Work*. Although our observations, backed-up by research, suggest that managers are often unwilling or unable to move beyond the task-specific conversation, rich conversations are a primary vehicle for improving the health of the working relationship between people at work and improving individual, team, and organizational performance.

Promoting a culture of conversation is a blend of skills and organizational climate. So in Part I, we consider the organizational climate and some of the barriers to developing a culture of conversation.

The **Top 10** Key Points …

1. By improving the quality (and frequency) of our conversations, managers have a practical, cost-effective, readily available communication vehicle to elevate the performance and well-being of organizational members, teams, enterprises, and, ultimately, society-at-large.

2. Managers in all industries the world over are reluctant to sit down with their charges and converse on important matters beyond essential task-specific activities and projects.

3. The health of the working relationship between people, particularly manager and employee, mostly depends on the quality and frequency of their interactions.

4. Managing the ebb and flow of conversations is a core skill of leadership.

5. There is a growing acceptance and understanding of the relevance and importance of conversations at work.

6. Organizations that thrive on dialogue typically have two underpinning aspects: a conducive climate and the right skills.

1 Pivotal leadership characterizes the complexity of coordinating the balance of being involved in multiple conversations about a range of matters and trying to make sense of these in shaping a constructive outcome.

8 Synching conversations is about the coordination of a host of inevitable conversations leaders have, or need to have, each with their unique tempo and speed.

9 As power shifts from positional authority to personal influence, managers will need to engage in more eclectic conversations and dialogue with employees, and an increasing array of stakeholders.

10 Due to their frequency and importance, there are economic, social, and psychological benefits in having better conversations.

part I

Developing a Culture
for Conversations

The "Them and Us" Employment Relationship: A Culture of Discouraging Conversations

The clear demarcation of roles and responsibilities and the unequal and overt power structures that supports this unwritten contract is an anathema to considered, constructive, and collaborative conversations.

A new employee was being inducted and trained by a long-time member of a customer service team. The new employee appreciated her trainer's experience and knowledge and quickly gained a level of confidence in her new role. One thing she also quickly learned was that a key performance measure was how quickly visitors were processed, not how well their inquiries were handled. "It feels like churn and burn," she told her trainer. "Lots of these people are coming back again and again with the same issue and they're upset at us for not giving them the right information. It seems like we should be spending more time finding out what the real issue is when they first come in." "Not our problem," said her trainer. "That's the manager's problem. They just don't want to see lines of people." Although she wasn't content with this, the new employee persevered with things until she took complete ownership of the role and then started engaging in richer conversations to try to prevent repeated visits and provide better customer service. "You're taking too long with the customers," she was told by her manager. Explaining her rationale and commitment to deliver better service was to no avail. "That's not your concern," she was told.

We could probably all identify a "them and us" employment relationship if we witnessed it ... and many of us have! But we want to give you a framework for conceptualizing and understanding the traditional employment relationship in this chapter. Of all the barriers to creating a culture of solution-focused, innovation-oriented, developmental conversations, the biggest obstacle is an outdated psychological contract between management and workforce where management refers to employees as *they* and employees refer to managers as *them*. So what is meant by the term *psychological contract*, and how is it relevant to promoting a conversation culture? Once you grasp this important connection, we can define the conventional working relationship. This traditional employment relationship has been in existence since the dawn of industry and its characteristics are still prevalent in many contemporary organizations.

The traditional employment relationship model is based on eight shared values between management and labor. In the next chapter (Chapter 3) we introduce you to the new employment relationship model. This employment relationship is diametrically opposite to the old "them and us" relationship we cover in this chapter. A new psychological contract is pivotal to organizations where meaningful conversation thrives, where ideas and innovation can flourish, because knowledge is not only shared but created; where issues can be dealt with constructively and rapidly because the drive to improve is stronger than the fear of failure.

But before we consider this new working relationship, we need to understand the 200-year-old employment relationship and its shortcomings for promoting healthy conversations in organizations. Both of these models are based on research.

Psychological contract

The psychological contract is basically a set of unwritten expectations between employees and managers. Historically, employees have had a reasonably fixed set of beliefs about the role of management. Similarly, managers have certain generalized expectations of the role of employee. The traditional employment relationship is based on a set of clear-cut beliefs from both entities about the role the other entity ought to play in the working relationship.

Employees, for example, generally have an expectation that they will be paid on time, treated with respect, and be given a fair go by organizational leaders. If, in the view of one or more employees with these basic beliefs, management doesn't uphold these ideas, then in the mind of those employees, the conventional psychological contract has been breached. In other words, management has failed to live up to their side of the unwritten agreement and consequently infringed the contract.

Equally, a manager with a customary belief about employees expects them to work hard, cause few problems, and arrive and leave work punctually. Again, if an employee's behavior is inconsistent with these expectations, they have violated the contract from the manager's perspective. These perspectives have been handed down from generation to generation, with little real substantial change. Where do most managers learn their management skills? From their managers. And who manages the managers? Those who were previously in those managers' roles.

Since the 1980s, the traditional psychological contract has been unraveling. Generally speaking, younger employees have vastly different expectations of work and of organizations than previous generations of employees typically had. For instance, the contemporary employee has an expectation that they will be involved in a meaningful way in the decision-making processes of the team and maybe of the organization. Traditional employees had a different set of beliefs that revolved around things like being given clear instructions on the work that needs to be done and no expectation of being involved in decision-making. We shouldn't limit this change of mindset only to *Gen Y* and *Gen X* employees compared to *Baby Boomers* either, because many of the Baby Boom generation have shifted their beliefs and expectations over the years in response to cultural change, education, and their own life circumstances.

The beliefs managers now have of employees are changing too. For instance, most managers now have an expectation that employees will demonstrate appropriate initiative when a situation warrants it. But pre-1980s, managers held a diametrically opposite expectation; that employees would – above all else – be compliant and obedient. The workplace is full of these changed and conflicting beliefs and expectations about the roles of management and labor. This lack of clarity around the emerging psychological contract leads to communication breakdowns and loss of trust between managers and employees.

Notwithstanding this confusion, the biggest impediment to cultivating a conversation culture is an adherence to the expectations of the traditional psychological contract; often characterized as a "them and us" relationship between management and labor. Despite the rhetoric in the popular management books, this "them and us" culture is still pretty much alive and well in organizational life. With a disproportionate power relationship between manager and employee, it is likely that the majority of conversations between a manager and employee that occur are perfunctory and task-specific. What's more, a traditional thinking manager, who still embraces the "them and us" psychological contract, will probably view meaningful, non-project specific dialogue as a pointless exercise.

From a traditional thinking employee's perspective, they will undoubtedly also shirk this type of interaction with their boss. They will avoid these types of conversations for two reasons. First, they probably don't see it as their role to have collaborative conversations with their boss. Second, having a relatively equal say on a host of matters with their boss is counter to their set of expectations of how the relationship should work. They may rationalize that the topics of these conversations are decisions that the manager ought to make without their input.

Briefly, managers who believe in the command and control management philosophy, supported by a traditional employment relationship, are not going to see the value in downing tools to have a shared conversation with their employees. And employees with a similar set of beliefs will probably see it the same way; they both believe it is the boss's role to get on and make the decision.

This outdated employment relationship is a significant roadblock to developing a conversation culture. But this barrier is exacerbated in circumstances where there is a misalignment between the employee's and manager's expectations.

Take, for example, Travis, a manager who has beliefs consistent with a new psychological contract. Travis is open to the idea of working with his employees in a collaborative relationship. His leadership style consequently is based on dialogue with his team when the situation calls for it. However, Jerry, one of Travis's team members, has a fairly traditional attitude about the employment relationship. Jerry holds the view that it is the manager's responsibility to make decisions; after all, in his mind, that is what the boss gets paid to do. Further, Jerry sees his role as getting on and doing what has been asked of him by the boss, in this case Travis. As a result of these conflicting expectations, Jerry views conversations and open dialogue with Travis as unnecessary and even a waste of time. These conflicting unwritten expectations result in some real frustration between Travis and Jerry, despite the fact that both are, in their own ways, trying to fulfil what they understand to be their responsibilities.

This works in reverse too. For example, Mary is an employee with an expectation that as part of a team she will be consulted and involved in decision-making from time-to-time on work-related issues. Further, Mary believes that Jenny, her manager, ought to share the responsibilities for decision-making with her team. But in this case, Jenny has a different understanding of the psychological contract to Travis's. Jenny thinks that the lines of responsibility between herself and her team are very clear. In Jenny's mind, her managerial role is broadly to make decisions and the team member's job is to follow her instructions and carry out the work. Mary finds it exasperating that Jenny is unwilling to engage the team in discussions. She is keen to discuss her ideas with Jenny. But Jenny is not at all receptive to any of her ideas or suggestions. Jenny doesn't believe in collaborative leadership. She views her role, and the role of all management, differently. Jenny thinks her role is to be decisive and to communicate those decisions clearly to employees. Jenny thinks of this as being accountable and professional. Mary labels this mindset as command and control. Proper conversations are hardly going to prosper in circumstances where there is a misalignment of expectations between manager and employee – and where each judges the other based on misaligned expectations. Once again, two well-intentioned people find themselves mutually locked out of a more productive working relationship because of conflicted psychological contracts.

Traditional psychological contract

Before discussing the new employment mindset conducive to a culture of conversation in the next chapter, let's come to terms with what is meant by the traditional employment relationship. The detailed description we are about to outline serves three useful purposes. First, it will assist in understanding the shortcomings of the "them and us" relationship in coping with a fast-moving, dynamic marketplace requiring constant dialogue between manager and employee. Second, it helps to sharpen the distinction between the old and new employment relationship. Third, it gives managers a set of useful benchmarks to measure progress towards a new working relationship that thrives on regular dialogue.

Table 2.1 below summarizes the attitudes of the traditional employment relationship from the perspective of both the employee and employer, based on eight shared values.

TABLE 2.1   Traditional employment relationship model[1]

Shared Value	Employee Mindset	Employer Mindset
Specialized Employment	*Work* in a clearly defined and specialized employment area.	*Offer* clearly defined and specialized employment opportunities.
Internal Focus	*Follow* organizational policies and practices.	*Reinforce* the need to follow organizational policies and practices.
Job Focus	*Fulfill* job requirements.	*Link* rewards and benefits to fulfilling job requirements.
Functional-Based Work	*Focus* on job functions.	*Structure* of work around functions.
Human Dispirit and Work	*Value* a stable and secure job.	*Offer* stable and secure jobs.
Loyalty	*Display* loyalty to the employer.	*Reward* employees who are loyal to the organization.
Training	*Commitment* to gain technical qualifications.	*Provide* opportunities for employees to develop technical skills.
Closed Information	*Comply* with managerial instructions.	*Provide* sufficient information for employees to do their job.

The left-hand column of Table 2.1 illustrates eight shared values based on research.[2] These values are characteristic of the traditional psychological contract. In the middle column, the eight brief descriptors summarize traditional managerial expectations of employees. If an employee breaches any of these expectations, traditional-thinking management will consider the contract dishonored. On the contrary, if employees are honoring these mindsets with consistent behavior, the value is reinforced. The right-hand column illustrates the traditional collective outlook of employees' expectations of management. From the perspective of the traditional-thinking employee, if any of these expectations are broken, employees will consider this a contract breach. On the other hand, if management's behavior is consistent with these mindsets, the values of the traditional employment relationship are strengthened. When these collective employee and management mindsets are enacted, the traditional psychological contract is perpetuated. And should any of these responses be violated by either partner in the employment relationship, the traditional psychological contract is broken temporarily or permanently.

At the heart of any human relationship is a process of exchange between two people. At its most basic level, the exchange in the traditional employment relationship consists of a manager specifying work requirements and – in return for a willingness to comply – the worker receives a wage. This has been the conventional lynchpin of the relationship between manager and employee since the birth of industry. Any failure to meet a work instruction, or pay the agreed wage, means the contract collapses. In this kind of rigid relationship, with clear roles and responsibilities, conversations will undoubtedly be limited to task-specific issues.

The traditional boss–worker relationship is easy to follow despite its shortcomings. It has worked successfully and has remained virtually unchanged for over 200 years. But organizations that are still operating under this employment relationship paradigm are increasingly less likely to adjust to the challenges and opportunities the global economy offers. The conventional psychological contract places unproductive constraints on people. The essence of the difficulty is this: while the traditional contract is simple, people are more complicated, and the work they do is increasingly complex.

This has long been known, of course, but industry seems to have done its best to resist and ignore the reality and the potential for changing the employment dynamic, because of the inherent challenges. Henry Ford was reputed to have once said, "Why is it every time I ask for a pair of hands they come attached to a brain?" Even if he didn't say it, the thought has been widely held!

In this traditional exchange process, managers are given responsibility and employees are set tasks. This creates a paradox. Employees who are not given responsibility never become responsible. The fewer people who take on responsibility, the greater the burden of accountability that falls on the shoulders of the manager. This process reinforces and perpetuates the "them and us" relationship paradigm. However, in reality, managers can disappoint and employees can surprise others by their initiative and enterprise.

Against the backdrop of a less predictable and stable marketplace, and of the increasing need for adaptability and innovation, the answer to resolving this dilemma would seem fairly obvious. Surely a less formal employment relationship, where managers provide employees with the freedom to be flexible and innovative in their approach to carrying out their work, is the way forward? This approach is widely advocated in many popular management books.

Unfortunately this new approach opens the door for some employees to manipulate the system. The overlapping areas of freedom can encourage unwelcome forms of initiative being shown by political operators. For instance, employees who display appropriate initiative may be quick to take credit for this. But on the other hand, they may cite a lack of clarity as the reason for not showing enterprise when expected to by their manager. These grey areas of employee autonomy are lessened in a prevailing traditional employment contract, as illustrated in Table 2.1. Put in simple terms: if it is not on the employee's job description, then it doesn't need to be done – and not doing something can be easily defended by the "work to rule" employee.

Some managers also undoubtedly feel threatened by a more fluid working relationship. The traditional-minded manager, feeling insecure about a more ambiguous arrangement or confronted by ambitious employees, will often revert to the simple separation of responsibilities characterized by the "them and us" relationship. This reaction to nullifying the freedom of employees further entrenches the traditional psychological contract.

So the challenge is to formulate a new working relationship with the same degree of clarity as the traditional employment relationship, but without the same inflexible separation of responsibility. That sounds like a paradox too! Unlike the traditional contract, managers will not delegate and supervise tasks to the same extent. Employees are expected to take greater responsibility and to be more accountable for their output. But unless the expectations are clear, simple, and accountable for both parties, any attempt to implement a new way of operating will lead to disagreement, frustration, and confusion.

The good news is the new model we propose has enormous advantages for both parties. The bad news is that there is increasingly little choice in breaking the "them and us" mindset. Employees with a modern mindset are likely to seek out meaningful work, engage in continuous lifelong learning, and assert their independence. Organizations populated with employees with these attitudes are likely to prosper if they are able to harness and sustain their energy. A workplace filled with independently-minded but cooperatively-minded employees working on tasks they find fulfilling is unquestionably a powerful competitive advantage for an enterprise. Companies with these types of employees are inevitably going to achieve higher levels of productivity and responsiveness to fluctuations in market conditions.

In conclusion, without a move away from this traditional psychological contract, it is hard to envisage a culture of genuine conversation. There will still be conversations in organizations based on the old psychological contract. But they are not the type of conversations we are endeavoring to encourage in this book. They will most likely be confined to superficial (but necessary) dialogue around task-specific activity. As we indicated at the outset of this chapter, the old "them and us" working relationship is the greatest impediment to promoting a culture of conversation. The clear demarcation of roles and responsibilities and the unequal and overt power structures that support this unwritten contract is an anathema to considered, constructive, and collaborative conversations. More specifically, the kinds of dialogues that will not happen in this culture are conversations to develop working relationships, conversations around personal growth and development, and conversations around collaborative decision-making and problem-solving. And on the chance they do take place, they are not going to be a sustainable feature of the landscape. We need a new working relationship with less rigidity and more collaboration for a conversation culture to take hold.

The next chapter introduces you to this new employment relationship as the foundation for creating and supporting a conversation culture.

The **Top 10** Key Points …

 1 The traditional employment relationship model is based on eight shared values and expectations between management and labor.

2 *Specialized Employment* means offering clearly defined and specialized employment opportunities and a willingness from employees to work in these jobs.

3 *Internal Focus* is about a willingness and reinforcement of the need to follow organizational policies and practices.

4 *Job Focus* means fulfilling and rewarding the requirements of the job.

5 *Functional-Based Work* is focusing and structuring work around functions.

6 *Human Dispirit and Work* is about no more than offering and valuing secure jobs.

7 *Loyalty* means displaying and being rewarded for loyalty to the organization.

8 *Training* refers to the commitment and provision of technical skills and qualifications, as distinct from other learning and development opportunities.

9 *Closed Information* means complying with managerial instructions based on sufficient but limited information.

10 A traditional psychological contract is an anathema to a culture of conversation.

3

A New Employment Relationship: A Culture of Encouraging Conversations

All relationships that work are based upon shared responsibility. Conversations are the catalyst for developing the employment relationship.

Research across the years suggests that it is at the too often neglected level of everyday conversation that the most powerful change interventions occur. Weick states: "The power of conversation, dialogue and respectful interaction to reshape ongoing change has often been overlooked. We are in thrall to the story of dramatic interventions in which heroic figures turn around stubbornly inertial structures held in place by rigid people who are slow learners. This is a riveting story. It is also a deceptive story. It runs roughshod over capabilities already in place, over the basics of change, and over changes that are already underway."[1]

We now turn our attention to a framework for a workplace culture built on an intentional commitment to open, two-way conversations. This culture is based on a new psychological contract between managers and employees. The contract is diametrically opposite to the traditional psychological contract illustrated in the last chapter.

Many organizations, from our observations, are in transition between the old and new psychological contracts. But as we mentioned at the outset of the last chapter, the traditional "them and us" relationship will, more than anything else, inhibit the promotion of a culture of conversation. And because the transition relies on rich conversations, trust, and the two-way flow of information towards a shared goal, the transition, far from happening automatically or seamlessly, will be fraught with resistance and frustration. The new employment relationship model we illustrate here provides you with some benchmarks to determine the extent to which your organization generally matches the new framework. The model, like the traditional employment relationship model, is based on eight shared values between employees and managers. Subsequently, we'll finish this chapter with some suggested conversations that are applicable for the eight underpinning values. These conversations will maintain and reinforce the new psychological contract. The model provides you with a roadmap for fostering the right culture for conversations to thrive in organizational settings you are part of.

New psychological contract

We have defined one end of the psychological contract continuum in the previous chapter. Now we move to the other end of the continuum to consider a diametrically opposite model. The research-based new employment relationship model takes into account the changing dynamics in the world of work and the changing requirements for organizations to survive and thrive. A workplace revolution began in the 1980s;[2] it profoundly changed the expectations employees and employers have of each other. The new model serves as a point of reference for organizations to capture the essence of these changes. A culture supported by the new employment relationship model is a culture based on and sustained by a wider and deeper range of conversations between managers and team members.

Table 3.1 below illustrates the eight shared values and the appropriate responses expected from employees and managers.

This new employment relationship model and the traditional employment relationship model introduced in the previous chapter, provide the polar benchmarks of the psychological contract. Both frameworks are based on eight shared values. The models describe a set of expectations employees and employers have of each other. Behaviors that are consistent or inconsistent with these collective

TABLE 3.1 New employment relationship model

Shared Value	Employee Mindset	Employer Mindset
Flexible Deployment	*Willingness* to work in a variety of organizational roles and settings.	*Encourage* employees to work in other organizational roles.
Customer Focus	*Serve* the customer before your manager.	*Provide* information, skills, and incentives to focus externally.
Performance Focus	*Focus* on what you do, not where you work.	*Link* rewards and benefits with performance rather than organizational dependency.
Project-Based Work	*Accept* yourself as a project-based worker rather than a function-based employee.	*Structuring* work around projects rather than organizational functions.
Human Spirit and Work	*Valuing* work that is meaningful.	*Provide* work (wherever possible) that is meaningful.
Commitment	*Commit* to assisting the organization achieve its outcomes.	*Commit* to assisting employees to achieve their personal objectives.
Learning and Development	*Commit* to lifelong learning.	*Enter* into a partnership for employee development.
Open Information	*Willing* to show enterprise and initiative.	*Providing* employees with access to a wide range of information.

mindsets will either reinforce or challenge the corresponding value in the left-hand column. It would be helpful to briefly illustrate the contrasting values between the two models.

Specialized employment to flexible deployment

The value of specialized employment is concerned with offering clearly defined and specialized employment opportunities in exchange for a readiness to work in a clearly defined and specialized employment area. Conversely, flexible deployment is defined as encouraging employees to work in other organizational roles in exchange for a willingness from employees to do so.

Internal focus to customer focus

Internal focus is essentially about reinforcing the need to follow organizational policies and procedures in exchange for readiness from employees to follow those policies and practices. Conversely, the value of customer focus is concerned with providing employees with information, skills, and processes to focus on the needs of the customer in exchange for employees serving the needs of customers wherever possible.

Job focus to performance focus

The value of job focus is linking benefits to employees fulfilling those job requirements. Conversely, performance focus is linking rewards and benefits in exchange for employees focusing on what needs to be done, over where they work.

Functional-based work to project-based work

Functional-based work is structuring work around organizational functions in exchange for employees focusing on their job function. Conversely, project-based work is structuring work around projects rather than organizational functions in exchange for employees accepting themselves as project-based workers rather than functional-based employees.

Human dispirit and work to human spirit and work

Human dispirit and work is based on the idea of offering stable and secure jobs in exchange for employees valuing stable and secure jobs. Conversely, human spirit and work is providing work, wherever possible, that is meaningful in exchange for employees valuing meaningful work opportunities.

A T   T H E   S C R E E N   F A C E ...

Enabling an ongoing company-wide conversation

US supermarket chain, SupaValu, began using Yammer in 2011 to connect more than 10,000 store managers and company executives. They formed more than 1000 online conversation groups that shared ideas and resolved challenges on an ongoing basis – something even a company-wide face-to-face retreat couldn't offer, and at a fraction of the cost.

"You've got to let the conversations happen, even if you might not like all of that conversation," CIO Wayne Shurts told *USA Today*. "It's going to happen around the water cooler anyway."[3]

Loyalty to commitment

Loyalty is concerned with rewarding employees who are loyal to the organization in exchange for employees displaying loyalty to their employer. Conversely, the value of commitment is about assisting employees to achieve their personal objectives in exchange for their commitment to assisting the organization in achieving its objectives.

Training to learning and development

Training in this sense is concerned with providing opportunities for employees to develop their technical skills in exchange for commitment to gain technical qualifications. Conversely, learning and development is entering into a partnership for employee development in exchange for a commitment to being a lifelong learner.

Closed information to open information

Closed information is providing sufficient information for employees so that they are able to do their jobs and, in exchange, employees complying with managerial instructions. Conversely, open information is providing employees with access to a wide range of information in exchange for the employees' willingness to show enterprise and initiative.

As you can see from these brief descriptors, the two sets of values in the models are diametrically opposite to each other; they provide the two ends of the psychological contract spectrum. How closely you and your organization are aligned to either model will dictate and reflect the type of organizational dialogue that is likely to occur between managers and team members.

Any human relationship is based on an exchange between two people. The employment relationship is no different to any other relationship in this regard. Expectations set the tone for the relationship. The contrasting expectations between the old and new psychological contracts will significantly shape the kind of relationship between the manager and team member. When behaviors and expectations are congruent, the boundaries of the relationship are formed. All relationships that work are based upon shared responsibility. Conversations are the vehicle for the formulation of all relationships.

In the context of the workplace, both the new and the traditional employment relationships models illustrate the mutual process of exchange and the associated responsibilities. This partnership is formed jointly by each party – the employee and the employer – fulfilling the requirements expected of them. Therefore, to satisfy the needs of both entities in moving to a new relationship, there has to be an appreciation of the new requirements and a clear understanding of how they can be met in the context of the changing workplace. If managers fail to understand and appreciate the changing needs of employees, they will doubtlessly not meet their expectations. Equally, if traditional-thinking employees are unfamiliar with changing needs of the modern organization, they will not be able to fulfill their obligations and meet the expectations of managers. Both parties now have a new set of accountabilities that need to be fulfilled to make the new employment relationship work.

A T   T H E   C O A L   F A C E   ...

The yin and yang

By way of an analogy, this individual/ organization interface can be likened to the "yin and yang" freedom dance. In a yin/yang relationship, both halves are incomplete and need each other to achieve the unified whole. In the same way, the model specifies eight values to guide a new employer/employee partnership. In this way, there is a co-dependency between individual and organization. By co-dependency we mean the individual and organization are wholly reliant upon each other. The employee and employer were co-dependent in the old employment relationship and they are co-dependent in the new. The difference is in what the relationship delivers to each party. One is predetermined and limited, the other is emergent and unlimited.

Managers and employees operating from conflicting mindsets will unquestionably be disappointed and frustrated with the signals they receive from the other partner in the relationship. For instance, an organizationally-dependent employee is less likely to be flexible with customer requests, particularly if doing so interferes with company policy. The traditional-thinking employee, confusing an act of compliance with a gesture of organizational loyalty, will disappoint a customer-focused boss. Likewise, a modern-thinking employee will find proactive behavior may be detrimental to their career in a bureaucratically-run organization. These misunderstandings – based on mismatched expectations about the employment relationship discussed in the previous chapter – occur on a daily basis in most workplaces, eroding trust levels and causing distress. Nevertheless, the challenge of these paradigm shifts, and the inevitable tension they bring, provide an opportunity for organizations to develop a new form of collaboration founded on the changing needs of employees and managers and their roles in personal and organizational success.

Mutual benefits for managers and employees

There are many benefits for both employee and employer in the new employment relationship paradigm. Specifically, Table 3.2 details these benefits with each value from the perspectives of employee and employer.

The employee benefits are linked to employability, development of new skills, greater job satisfaction, and more autonomy to make decisions. These advantages are consistent with the changing attitudes and expectations of skilled, confident, and well educated employees. Therefore, employees who have these mindsets are likely to want to work in organizations that foster these values. The organizational benefits are greater flexibility, responsiveness, and maneuverability in the marketplace. These advantages are also consistent with changing employer needs. Consequently, employers

TABLE 3.2   Benefits of the new employment relationship model

Shared Value	Benefits to Employee	Benefits to Employer
Flexible Deployment	*Learn* a variety of skills and competencies to enhance employability within and outside the organization.	*Enhance* maneuverability to respond faster to changing market forces.
Customer Focus	*Enhance* customer engagement skills to improve employability.	*Retain* and *increase* market share.
Performance Focus	*Rewarded* for increased value to the organization.	*Increased* productivity.
Project-Based Work	*Develop* team building skills and *add* variety and interest beyond functional role.	*Improve* ability to respond quickly to challenges and opportunities in the marketplace.
Human Spirit and Work	*Gain* greater satisfaction and meaning from work.	*Retain* key staff and corporate knowledge.
Commitment	*Build* career capabilities.	*Instill* greater commitment from employees to achieve organizational outcomes.
Learning and Development	*Broaden* the array of skills and competencies beyond the scope of current job.	*Grow* and *develop* the organization.
Open Information	*Improve* capacity to make a greater organizational contribution.	*Increase* responsiveness through quicker decision-making processes.

who promote these values are likely to attract and retain employees with a complementary mindset.

We see the two concepts of the employment relationship and good constructive dialogue as a "chicken and egg" situation: what comes first? Without a new employment relationship that mirrors Table 3.1, it is not likely that collaborative conversations will occur in any permanent way or, if they do, they will be done sparingly. On the other hand, a new working relationship can only be sustained and developed through collaboration, dialogue, and conversation. Despite this paradox, we would strongly suggest that without a commitment and deliberate move toward a new psychological contract, widespread, sustained, significant conversations won't take place. As we pointed out at the beginning of this chapter, the dominant psychological contract in the organization will have a major bearing on what type and quality of conversation occurs.

To illustrate the point about the conversation being the powerhouse in supporting and strengthening a new employment relationship, we briefly consider each of the eight new values as a catalyst for conversations between managers and employees.

Types of conversations

The types of conversations we are referring to can be categorized as one of the following:

- Conversations to develop people.
- Conversations to build relationships.
- Conversations to make and review decisions.

We will cover each of these categories of conversation in more depth in Part II. But for now, we will use these three types of conversations to consider them in the context of the eight values of the new employment relationship.

Flexible deployment

The conversations around flexible deployment are mostly about developing people and taking action or making decisions. For instance, managers and employees need to have conversations on expanding skills-sets and providing feedback on how effectively those skills-sets are being attained. Briefly, these conversations are concerned with developing skills.

Customer focus

The conversations around customer focus are concerned with making decisions and taking action. For instance, to maintain a customer focus – that is, everything that is said, done, and thought about ought to have the customer in mind – regular discussions need to occur around the customer's welfare. Conversations around role conflict for customer service employees need to be resolved. Critical incidents that went well or not so well are open for conversations too, as a means of improving the customer experience.

Performance focus

Conversations around performance are inevitably about developing people. A performance focus value requires feedback and dialogue between a manager and their team members. By feedback, we mean entering into a dialogue regarding whether KPIs have been met and, if so, how can they be sustained? And if not, what can be done to improve performance?

Project-based work

Project-based work requires conversations around building relationships, making decisions, and taking action. Moving from a functional-based to project-based organizational structure involves breaking down the formal, hierarchical channels of communication and replacing them with team-based discussions. In a project-based environment, cross-functional dialogue becomes more important than formal hierarchical channels of communication. Project teams also are designed to solve problems and take action.

Human spirit and work

Capturing the hearts and minds of employees mostly requires conversations around building relationships and developing people. Human spirit and work is based on the degree to which someone is engaged in their organizational work. Research demonstrates that the level of engagement of an employee is largely dependent on the quality of the professional working relationship the employee has with their manager. Regular conversations are a vehicle for building this working relationship.

Commitment

Building commitment from employees is dependent on developing people and making decisions. Commitment is based on an exchange; that is, the organization provides the employee with developmental opportunities in exchange for a commitment to work toward the goals and objectives of the organization. To do this effectively, managers and employees need to discuss, on the one hand, the needs of the employee in terms of their development and, on the other hand, regular discussions need to take place on the needs of the organization in terms of its strategic direction.

Learning and development

Learning and development conversations revolve around developing people. The concept of learning and development is a broader frame of reference than training, and is facilitated by the manager entering into regular dialogue with each employee to establish and make possible their individual growth needs.

Open information

Conversations that open up the channels of communication are required to make decisions based on timely and relevant information and taking appropriate action. The new employment relationship more than anything else is about improving the frequency, openness, and quality of information shared between the employee and manager. To do this effectively, it is expected that managers will have regular dialogue with employees to align and re-align the needs and interests of the individual and the organization.

So hopefully you can see that promoting a conversation culture without a new working relationship between managers and employees is problematic. What's more, a new employment relationship is the foundation for encouraging meaningful conversations in the workplace. The first step to transition from the traditional employment relationship to a new working relationship is to benchmark the extent to which the organization mirrors the two polar opposite models in this and the last chapter. The organization then needs to take active steps towards creating a new working relationship that is consistent with the new employment relationship model. And the new employment relationship and the eight supporting values are largely maintained through timely, relevant, and regular conversations between managers and employees. These conversations are about building trusting working relationships, developing employees, or making collaborative decisions where appropriate.

In the next chapter, the final chapter for Part I, we look at other barriers beside the traditional employment relationship that can impede conversations in the workplace.

The **Top 10** Key Points ...

1. Like the traditional employment relationship model, the new employment relationship model is based on eight shared values and expectations between management and labor.

2. *Flexible Deployment* is encouraging employees to work in other organizational roles and a willingness from employees to do so.

3. *Customer Focus* is providing information, skills, and incentives to focus externally and for employees to serve the customer before their manager.

4. *Performance Focus* is linking rewards and benefits with performance rather than organizational dependency, and for employees to focus on what they do, not where they work.

5. *Project-Based Work* is structuring work around projects rather than organizational functions, and for employees to accept themselves as project-based workers rather than functional-based employees.

6. *Human Spirit and Work* is the provision of work (wherever possible) that is meaningful, and for employees to value work that is meaningful.

7. *Commitment* is based on committing to assist employees to achieve their personal objectives in exchange for a commitment from employees to assist the organization to achieve its outcomes.

8. *Learning and Development* is based on the organization entering into a partnership for employee development, and for the employee to commit to lifelong learning.

9 *Open Information* is providing employees with access to a wide range of information, and for employees to be willing to show enterprise and initiative.

10 The new employment relationship is the catalyst for creating a culture of conversation.

4

The Nine Common Barriers to Communication

Attention is the price we pay for insight, understanding, critical thinking, learning, and successful action.

A manager on a communication course led by one of the authors realized that his conversations with his staff were far more limited than was healthy. He had somehow found himself trapped by the organizational culture and structures that deliberately separated managers from the people they managed. He saw himself as an "open door" manager, approachable and friendly, but was puzzled why people rarely came to him – and why when he initiated conversations with them they were often initially guarded and even suspicious. He guessed it must just be that "manager–staff gulf." The conversations during the course highlighted the fact that something as mundane as the physical location of his office was actually influencing the way he was perceived and how approachable he was. The office he had inherited when he became the manager was at the back of the work area, so staff visiting from other offices or sites, particularly, had to negotiate all the other workstations and then his assistants before actually reaching him, way at the back in his spacious and private area. When he came back for a follow-up workshop a month later, he reported that he had moved his office further towards the front entry so that he was more visible and accessible. And suddenly more of his staff were stopping by to share information.

We've looked at the significant role psychological barriers play in hindering effective conversations, particularly the unwritten contract between employee and employer. We'll now look at nine other widespread barriers in organizations that prevent or inhibit the flow of information through conversations.

Briefly, the nine barriers are:

1. Inattention during conversations.
2. Restricted information channels.
3. Lack of feedback.
4. A culture of not asking questions.
5. Too much formality.
6. Overreliance on email.
7. Lack of role models.
8. A fear of emotion.
9. Physical office lay-out.

There are undoubtedly more barriers to consider. But these nine are the main barriers that discourage conversations in our opinion.

Removing – or at least managing – these nine barriers is important to enhancing the quality of organizational communication between people. In her book, *Energize Your Workplace*, Professor Jane Dutton reminds us that:

> Managers and leaders shape possibilities for energy in connection through two important means: how they interact with others and how they design and construct the contexts in which others interact ... The energy and vitality of individuals and organisations alike depends on the quality of the connections among people in the organisation.[1]

The obstacles to energy and vitality that Dutton refers to can be personal, structural, cultural, procedural, or physical. We invite you to consider each of these barriers in relation to the organizations you work in.

Barrier 1: Inattention

We've all found ourselves nodding distractedly as someone is talking to us. We're sort of listening – or maybe just hearing them – but our attention is limited because other things are in view, on our minds, or in our hearing. The result is "fragmented attention" – everyone gets a little, but no one really gets it all.

One of the most significant ways we "spend" our time is through how we "pay" attention. Attention is the price we pay for insight, understanding, critical thinking, learning, and successful action. The trouble is, managing our attention is a constant challenge. There's simply too much information, too few hours, and too little energy with which to pay attention to everything. Managing our own attention is an essential first step in genuinely communicating effectively with others.

Warren Bennis identified "management of attention" as one of the four key competencies of 90 of the top business and public sector leaders in the US.[2] One of the people he most wanted to interview was also one of the hardest for him to get an appointment with – the renowned pianist, musicologist, and conductor, Leon Fleischer. Not long before Bennis finally managed to secure an interview (it took a couple of years), he happened to speak to two of Fleischer's students at a music festival. He asked them about what made Fleischer so effective and respected. "I'll tell you what makes him so great," said one of the students. "He doesn't waste our time."

Later, as Bennis not only spoke with Fleischer but also observed his rehearsal and class work he saw this assessment in action. "Every moment Fleischer was before the orchestra, he knew exactly what sound he wanted. He didn't waste time because his intentions were always evident."

Investing intentional attention where it matters leads to effective communication that results in productive action.

Attention is a discipline – and one that for most of us is a constant struggle. So it can help to remember some basic principles about managing this precious resource as we communicate.

Reduce manageable distractions

Email, telephone, and social media alerts interrupt and distract us from the people we are attempting to communicate with. Turn them off and focus on them properly after you've had your conversation. Constantly checking your smart phone is a classic form of self-distraction. Likewise, having too many things in your mental to-do list is like having a barrel of live monkeys on your desk – something is guaranteed to jump out and demand attention midway through a conversation with someone, whether it's important or not.

Focus on one conversation at a time

Even if it's only for a few minutes, directing your complete attention exclusively to the task-at-hand enables you to extract the maximum benefit of your mental effort, physical presence, and emotional energy. It's efficient – but creative, analytical, critical attention requires focus. If you're trying to attend to everything, you'll attend to nothing. Contrary to popular myth, we don't multi-task – the best we can do with cognitive tasks is to switch between tasks, which has the effect of slowing down our mental processes. It's inefficient. It's also destructive when it comes to showing respect to others and to genuine listening and understanding. One way to assess your focus is to ask "how present am I in this conversation?"

Identify your most attentive times of the day

Few of us can completely control our schedules, but most of us are aware of those times when we struggle most to pay focused attention to others. Whether it's the start of the day, the end of the day, or after lunch for you, if you know when your resources are most frayed you can probably avoid those conversations you know are going to require a more alert mental state.

Your attention is a valuable and limited resource. If you lead others, your attention is also a reliable guide to them as to what is important and valued. So where, when and how you invest your attention is, as the late Warren Bennis observed, a key leadership competency.

Your attention is a valuable and limited resource. If you lead others, your attention is also a reliable guide to them as to what is important and valued.

Barrier 2: Restricted information channels

A lack of timely and relevant information in an organization is going to stifle discussion. "You'll get told on a need to know basis" is a common refrain from managers who embrace the traditional psychological contract. This belief will not lead to the fostering of a conversation culture. Being told on a need to know basis generates rumors, gossip, and innuendo; the opposite outcome of an organization that thrives on healthy conversations. This is because as human beings we crave certainty. And, especially in times of change, when we are uncertain we will take whatever certainty is on offer – even if it's incomplete, ill-informed, or just plain inaccurate information.

The less inclined managers are to communicate important information, the more it inhibits meaningful conversations. Some conversations still occur, but they are the wrong conversations. They are likely to be underground conversations based on half-truths and inaccuracies between employees, away from management. Without open information, open conversations are not going to take place. Opening the information channels is the catalyst for facilitating dialogue between people at work.

So if it makes so much sense, why don't we do it? The justification for a *you'll be told on a need to know basis* attitude is the perceived risk of open communication. Managers with this traditional mindset believe the risks outweigh the advantages. What are these risks? The risk is that this information could be used for the wrong purposes. It may be "leaked" to the media, conveyed to the union, or circulated to customers; briefly, it will get into the wrong hands.

A closed information organization is based on two false assumptions. In failing to open up communication channels, traditional managers assume that employees can't be trusted with this information. Further, those employees may pass sensitive information on to inappropriate sources. This is misguided. The false assumption here is that managers can be more trusted with confidential information. Sometimes they can and, equally, sometimes they can't. At its heart, the assumption for not sharing information is this: We trust management to not misuse information, but we don't trust employees to not leak the information or use it in a negative way. Granted, there are many more employees than managers and perhaps the risk is that, with larger numbers, the abuse of this information is greater. But the idea that employees are less trustworthy than management is erroneous. That false belief is not lost on employees either; they know that this is symbolic of a lack of trust. And this does nothing to build a trusting and a collaborative environment. The second false assumption is that by withholding information you can control it. This is flawed in two ways. One we've already noted, in that information vacuums will be filled with some sort of information – which invites a risk greater than that of sharing accurate information. The other is that social media and networked organizations mean very little information can actually be locked away.

Opening up the information channels does not need an elaborate organizational communication plan or a new department. It simply needs managers to be willing and able to have open, honest conversations in which they share as much information as they can. Naturally, there will be information that for privacy, commercial-in-confidence, or other legitimate reasons cannot be shared or cannot be shared in full from time-to-time. Everyone appreciates that. But even being willing to explain that "I'm telling you everything I'm in a position to tell you right now" or "That's as much information as I've been given right now" communicates openness and trust.

And of course it's a two-way street. If managers aren't willing to share information with their teams, how likely are those same team members to share information with their managers? Especially if the information is challenging or negative.

Every organization pays "ignorance tax," says management writer Gary Hamel.[3] Ignorance tax is levied on managers and on team members every time information is withheld. Which makes restricted information channels a prime target for improving the quality of organizational communication.

Barrier 3: Lack of feedback

Closely associated with a lack of open information is a culture that doesn't believe in regular feedback. Not giving feedback reduces trust levels. And the opposite is also true: a feedback-rich environment builds trust through understanding. In an organization that is starved of feedback, employees don't know where they stand and clarity and direction suffers as a result.

Feedback in these environments is limited to static conversations. Conversations are limited to work-related projects. Most of this dialogue is of course essential, but it hardly constitutes constructive dialogue. Most of the communication centers around reporting, problems, fault finding, and updates. Conversations around enhancing relationships, problem-solving (solutions), and taking strategic action are cast aside. Oral and written didactic reporting processes are the order of the day. Why? Because, despite its limited effectiveness, this type of dialogue is safe and relatively predictable.

A culture of continuous feedback necessitates a different type of dialogue and mutual discussion. By feedback we are referring to two-way feedback: from managers to employees and from employees to managers. The feedback can be positive or negative, but it is regular and ongoing. Such conversations create a culture of feedback that normalizes the process rather than limiting it to occasional formal, scripted exchanges. These feedback conversations are based on mutual respect and trust.

AT THE COAL FACE...

Why do we need feedback?

One of the authors recalls consulting to a well-known international orchestra several years ago. The author's role as a consultant was to increase the leadership literacy of the principal musicians who were the leaders of their sections.

The author mistakenly thought that the best starting point was to hold a series of conversations around the orchestra, going from section to section. He started each meeting with a simple enough question: "What would you like to see more of from your leaders?" The response overwhelmingly was "more feedback"; they wanted more feedback from their leaders.

Feeling reasonably confident, he convened a meeting of the principals and informed them of his findings from these discussions. A member of the orchestra, coming close to his retirement, replied in response to the author's comment that the musicians wanted more feedback: "Feedback! Why would they want more feedback? They have all passed their trial [like a probationary period in the corporate world], surely that is all the feedback they need."

The author was rendered speechless!

A brief word about the old "feedback sandwich" might be in order here. You know, "here's the positive … now here's a negative … and now here's a pat on the back to walk out the door with." It might sound good, but in practice we know the effect: "Here's the positive" … *("OK, what does my manager really want to talk to me about?")* … "Now here's the negative" … *("Ha! Why couldn't you just ask me about that instead of trying to sugar-coat it?")* … "And now here's a pat on the back to walk out the door with" … *("I'm still thinking about your criticism …")*. The positives are devalued because they are heard as simply polite ways of telling us off, and the lasting impression is that we've screwed up.

Why not, instead, look for opportunities to give positive feedback? And just leave it at that. Recognition, appreciation, and acknowledgment are simple, everyday opportunities to build a culture of positive feedback, into which occasional performance improvement conversations can become supportive and "matter-of-fact" experiences, rather than occasions to be avoided or endured.

Barrier 4: A culture of not asking questions

Many organizational leaders are attuned to answering questions rather than asking questions. This is particularly the case with professionals such as accountants, engineers, and lawyers. These professionals have all been taught to expertly answer questions, but not necessarily how to ask them. They are trained problem-solvers. Solutions to problems are predicated on responses to questions. As these technical experts get promoted into managerial roles they often take with them this mindset. Further, they struggle with the idea of asking questions. Technically-trained managers are more comfortable answering questions from others, including their employees and various stakeholders. But it is hardly possible to have a free-flowing conversation without asking questions.

The sort of questions we are referring to begin with words such as *why, what, where, how, which*, and *who*. These are open-ended questions. They encourage the other person in the conversation to elaborate on their utterances. These same technically-capable professionals are very good at answering these open-ended questions.

On the other hand, we have found that good leaders are very good at opening up dialogue. They use open-ended questions all the time to encourage conversation. "I am curious, *why* did you say that?" Or, "*what* do you mean?" Or, "*how* would that work in practice?" The other person feels compelled to elaborate.

Dr Michael Marquardt, in his book, *Leading with Questions*, writes that:

> When we become leaders we feel that it is important for us to have answers rather than questions ... The ability to ask questions goes hand in hand with the ability to learn. A learning organization is only possible if it has a culture that encourages questions.[4]

We observe many team meetings across a range of industry groups. It is rare to find managers posing thought-provoking questions at these meetings. And because of this, stimulating conversation in team meetings is a rarity. Most team meetings are the opposite: sterile, didactic affairs. Put another way, the meetings we often witness are usually mindless reporting processes that do nothing to stimulate conversation. The majority of "participants" at these meetings sit mutely through the ritual and have little or no input.

The power of questions is that they "serve as the foundation for increasing individual, team, and organizational learning. Every question can be a potential learning opportunity," says Marquardt. This is because questions cause our brains to work harder by making more neural connections. You can see the benefits for one-on-one, team, and even organizational conversations if people's brains are working to find new connections rather than simply searching for existing answers that may be out-of-date or unsuitable.

Barrier 5: Too much formality

Too much formality also stifles conversation. We see this a lot in bureaucratically-run organizations and in military and paramilitary organizations such as policing. Hierarchy is overemphasized and consequently the power relationship is upheld and respected above all else. In these formalized environments, the boss is always right, or at least that is the impression. People are told what to do; performance is simply about following instructions or responding to orders.

On the rare occasion that conversations do take place, they are usually embroiled with copious paperwork and procedural discussions. Employees are not encouraged to think for themselves, to display initiative, and show enterprise. Instead, employees are encouraged or coerced into following the boss's direction without question. Rewards and recognition are based on compliance rather than initiative. Ironically, we have found that senior managers of these formal organizations are perplexed and frustrated when their internal engagement surveys reflect a lack of trust and absence of accountability and ownership for decisions amongst more junior staff.

Managers in these rigid regimes are worried about maintaining order and power and not losing control. Managers are rewarded for being decisive and making quick decisions. Subordinates are rewarded for following directions and conforming to established practices. This type of culture negates the need for meaningful dialogue and rich conversations.

And while there are obvious benefits to using power, structures, and hierarchies for decision-making and communication in critical situations, there are clearly dangerous potential results too.

Consider how the airline industry found the need to develop what is known as "crew resource management" systems to encourage and enable subordinates in the cockpit to speak up when indicators suggested a problem the captain may not have seen or overlooked.

When the (US) National Transportation Safety Board (NTSB) investigated airline accidents in the 1970s, they:

> detected a culture and work environment in the cockpit that, rather than facilitating safe transportation, may have contributed to the accidents. The Board found that some captains treated their fellow cockpit crewmembers as underlings who should speak only when spoken to. This intimidating atmosphere actually led to accidents when critical information was not communicated among cockpit crewmembers.[5]

In its recommendations, the NTSB directed all carriers to:

> urge their assigned operators to ensure that their flight crews are indoctrinated in principles of flight deck resource management, with particular emphasis on the merits of participative management for captains and assertiveness training for other cockpit crewmembers.[6]

This became the foundation for crew resource management (CRM) – a system of risk management, problem-solving, and decision-making that emphasizes the need for situational awareness, teamwork, and communication within hierarchical team structures.

Barrier 6: Overreliance on email

Email is a wonderful tool when it is used properly. We all wonder how we coped in the days of pre-email. But too often email, like other technologies, is abused and not used in the right way. Instead of having a conversation, managers will often fire off emails to their staff asking for responses to their proposals. They are surprised and disappointed when they get little or no response to what they mistakenly think is an open communication style.

It's not that email is inherently bad, just that it has significant limitations when it comes to communicating effectively. Consider a few:

- It is limited to marks on a screen. No social context, no nonverbals, no visuals, no tone of voice (except the "tone" interpreted by the reader). It all makes email a very narrow, constrained communicational channel that creates strong potential for misinterpretation.
- It is asynchronous. The sending and receiving do not occur in sync with each other; they may occur minutes, hours, days, or even weeks apart.
- It is over-used. Because we are all swamped with email messages, it is natural and easy for us to ignore, overlook, or avoid incoming email – especially if it is not immediately clear why or how it is relevant to us.

The use of email is great for confirming what has taken place in a conversation and conveying information to a lot of people in a short space of time. But email is more often than not used as a poor substitute for constructive dialogue. This is often done on the premise that it saves valuable time. But a quick conversation about the very topic the manager is using email for can sometimes be quicker, more affirming, more engaging, and more effective. By conversing rather than emailing, managers are adopting a more collaborative leadership style rather than a directive leadership style.

There is an enormous difference between understanding a message and being committed to it. Email may do a fair job – if written well – to convey a message and deepen understanding, assuming of course that it is read! But a conversation does more than that. It can build an emotional connection and this may help employees gain a greater commitment to the issues at hand.

Improving communication, the key to tapping the value of social technology

There's no doubt technology opens up significant opportunities for overcoming some of the everyday barriers to richer workplace conversations. But technology in itself is not the answer, as noted in a McKinsey report into how to unlock the potential of the "social economy":

"Two-thirds of the value creation opportunity afforded by social technologies lies in improving communications and collaboration within and across enterprises. By adopting these organizational technologies, we estimate that companies could raise the productivity of knowledge workers by 20 to 25 percent. However, realizing such gains will require significant transformations in management practices and organizational behaviour."[7]

Barrier 7: Lack of role models

For good conversations to frequently occur in organizational settings, people need to see managers role modeling dialogue. In other words, employees need to see meaningful conversations in action. This may mean participating in those conversations or simply observing managers taking the time to have these conversations with others. The simple idea here is based on the adage that leaders set the tone. And if managers are seen to be willingly and continually engaging in dialogue, other organizational members will follow suit.

The opposite scenario is true too: if no one in the business is role modeling rich conversation, there is no exemplar; no illustration of how it ought to be. People at work need to see conversation in action to appreciate its value and impact. If people use the excuse that they are too busy to converse – which is code for "it's not important" – no amount of training and rhetoric about conversations will matter. They won't happen without role modeling from senior management. It starts with the CEO. If they are not showing the way, the senior management team will copy the behavior they observe. The pattern is repeated and cascades throughout the organization.

It's not enough for managers to say that their door is always open – what we want to know is whether their mind is open. It's not enough to say we value people's input – we need to experience input being valued through focused attention, interest, and response. Role modeling is essential because as human beings we trust what we see far more than what we are told. We look for evidence. That's what role modeling does – one way or the other.

The conversational leader engages in conversations everywhere and at any time with anybody. Some of these conversations are planned, others impromptu. Some are done in their office, others outside the office. They are part of this type of leader's style and approach. But for this to flourish across an organization, it requires more than one senior leader to lead by example.

Barrier 8: A fear of emotion

We believe that one of the main – and often unspoken – reasons why managers don't indulge in conversations is the fear of opening up a "can of worms." Managers worry about the emotional dimension. Specifically: How will people react? What do I do when others react emotionally? These are often uncomfortable questions for leaders. What if there are tears? What if they get upset? How will

I manage an aggressive response? These are often the questions that inhibit conversations, particularly the tougher conversations. Conversations can – and do – elicit emotion, and the world of work likes to pretend it is based purely on rationality, logic, and the non-emotional dimension.

Managers generally don't feel equipped to handle emotions in the workplace. Mechanisms are put in place to control and suppress feelings in organizations. For instance, reports and meetings with tight agendas are commonplace. These set pieces are inhibitors for having emotionally honest conversations. It is considered safer to stick to the script. This means managers more often than not use clinical communication channels – and language – that cut out the risk of opening up emotional content.

But it is delusional to assume that managers can remove feelings from the workplace. They can be avoided, ignored, or bypassed, but that doesn't mean that feelings and emotional influences are removed. What happens usually is that these feelings are bottled up and contribute to stress and tension in the workplace. They are then released in counterproductive or destructive ways. Meaningful conversations are a combination of content and emotion.

Charles Darwin, author of *Origin of the Species*, also wrote a book entitled *The Expression of Emotions in Man and Animals*, in 1872. He classified six universal emotions: happiness, sadness, fear, anger, surprise, and disgust. These are, as Darwin and others have indicated, fundamental to the human experience and to our communication. And yet, workplaces too often try to maintain the fiction that at work we must "switch off" our emotions. In fact, whether we demonstrate our emotional states or not, they are constantly playing a part in our decision-making, relationships, and communication. It is important to manage our emotional reactions (and emotional states), but part of being emotionally intelligent is being able to understand and appropriately respond to emotions – our own and others'. It's no accident that one of the most influential areas of leadership development in the last ten to 20 years has been in understanding how to manage and develop emotional intelligence.

Barrier 9: Physical office lay-out

The physical lay-out of any working environment is seriously under-estimated in terms of its impact on the culture of an organization. Although there may be very little you can do in terms of your current physical surroundings, planning for the future can be an important consideration for the type of culture a leader wants to promote.

Specifically, there are two important physical considerations that affect culture in the workplace. These are proximity and physical barriers. Proximity refers to the relative physical distance between people. In terms of physical lay-out, this means the distance between offices and where people are situated. The further some-one is from the center of the action, the more likely they are to be less involved and engaged in the day-to-day operations. For instance, being situated on another floor from the business hub will mean less traffic to and from that employee. And this means that others may consider it would be much quicker to send an email than visit them in person. This is made worse when someone works in a regional office or even another country. The old adage "out of sight, out of mind" becomes routine.

How often do we hear stories of people claiming in the regions that "head office doesn't understand the problems we face" or "we never see anyone from head office." Proximity affects the degree of face-to-face contact people have with each other and therefore affects the amount of conversing that is done.

The other office lay-out barrier is less subtle and involves physical barriers. This may include doorways, hallways, and secretaries or assistants who serve as gatekeepers. These barriers inhibit impromptu contact, often deliberately. For instance, a manager who adopts a closed-door rather than open-door policy sends a powerful signal that, unless it is really important, you are not to disturb me. Although we believe managers ought to have an open-door policy, we understand that at times it is prudent to close the door. But a manager who always has their door closed will have less contact with their team, either by accident or by design.

A hallway may present a different kind of obstacle. The hallway may be imposing and therefore not terribly inviting. This again can inhibit face-to-face contact. And a secretary is often referred to as a "gatekeeper" for good reason. They view their job as someone who protects the boss from being interrupted by others. After all, a gatekeeper is there to stop people idly walking into the office of the manager and having an impromptu conversation.

On the other hand, open-plan offices tend to stimulate more conversations. It is easy to walk up to someone and start a conversation in these lay-outs. Although it should be said that open-plan offices can also be a source of annoyance. Employees can – and often do – get interrupted for trivial reasons.

The lay-out of the office can either promote or inhibit a culture of conversation. Organizational leaders need to get the balance right. Recognizing the need for privacy and for "thinking time" should not discourage impromptu conversations from taking place. Does your workplace get this balance right?

We have looked at nine barriers that smother conversations in the workplace. Most of these barriers are based on the attitude of managers and how they view their role. An important step in cultivating a conversational organization is to remove – or at least manage – as many of these barriers as practically possible.

This concludes Part I. In Part II, we cover in more detail the three types of conversations we seek to promote more of in the changing organization.

The **Top 10** Key Points ...

1. Beyond the outdated psychological contract, the nine barriers to conversations are inattention during conversations, restricted information channels, lack of feedback, a culture of not asking questions, too much formality, overreliance on email, lack of role models, a fear of emotion, and physical office lay-out.

2. Managing our own attention is an essential first step in genuinely communicating effectively with others.

3. A lack of timely and relevant information in an organization is going to stifle discussion; actively withholding it will communicate distrust and discourage others from sharing information.

4. Closely associated with a lack of open information is a culture that doesn't believe in regular feedback. Not giving feedback reduces trust levels and misses the opportunity to encourage and appreciate good performance.

5. Many organizational leaders are attuned to answering questions rather than asking questions. A culture of not asking questions can be a barrier to conversations and will limit organizational learning.

6. Too much formality also stifles conversation by emphasizing the power distance between people.

7. An overreliance on email can be a barrier to conversation because it is a "lean" communication channel, is asynchronous, and often unclear.

8. For good conversations to frequently occur in organizational settings, people need to see managers role modeling dialogue. Culture is about the way things are done.

9. One of the main – and often unspoken – reasons why managers don't indulge in conversations is the fear of opening up a "can of worms" when people respond emotionally. But this ignores the reality of those emotions in people's thinking, decisions, and responses.

10. The physical lay-out of any working environment is seriously underestimated in terms of its potential impact on the culture of an organization through the way it facilitates or restricts conversations.

part II

Types of Workplace Conversations

5

Development Conversations: The Five Conversations Framework

Traditional performance reviews are not what we classify as developmental conversations; instead of performance development, performance reviews are essentially about performance assessment.

Craig was about to start the developmental conversation with Mary, one of his supervisors. He had arranged to meet Mary for this discussion in a quiet, comfortable room away from his office.

Craig had frequently been told about – and had observed several times first-hand – the unnecessarily abrupt way in which Mary spoke to her team members when she wanted something done. Craig felt that this was one area that required improvement. Mary was inclined to tell people what to do rather than ask them, and her team members resented this. Craig was concerned that Mary might not accept this criticism. He was a bit apprehensive about this conversation with Mary.

Mary arrived on time and Craig started with the question: "Mary, you've no doubt had a chance to review your current role. If there is one area in which you believe you have an opportunity for growth, what is it?" After a lengthy pause, she replied, "I can't seem to get my team members to show any initiative. I have to do all the thinking for them."

Craig replied: "Okay. Can you elaborate on this so that I understand what you mean?" "Well, I find myself telling people what to do when I would rather they show initiative and do what they are paid to do," said Mary. "What do you think the reason for this is, Mary?" "I don't know really," came Mary's reply.

"What are the consequences of this?" asked Craig. "Well I find I have to raise my voice and direct people to do what they should know already," Mary responded in an agitated voice. "When you raise your voice, what happens?" asked Craig. "People walk off in a huff usually and don't listen to me." "I see. I guess you're not happy about this reaction, then?" Craig probed. "No, I'm not at all."

"What would you like to happen?" asked Craig. "I would like them to listen to me and just do what needs to be done without any argument." "Well, what can you do differently to get this result?"

"Well, I don't know really."

"Have you tried asking them without raising your voice?" Craig suggested. "Yeah, but that doesn't work," Mary countered.

"When was the last time you did this?" "I can't remember. I get so frustrated. I can't help raising my voice." "But you say that's not working?" Craig replied patiently. "No, it definitely doesn't work, but it's the only way."

"Can I suggest you try asking them in a calm manner and see what happens? It's worth a go, isn't it?" "Well, nothing else is working, Craig!" Mary responded, exasperated.

"So I have your commitment to give it another try?" "Yeah, I suppose so," sighed Mary.

"Is there anything I can do to help?" "No, not really. You've been helpful just listening to me. I'll just have to control myself and do as you suggest." "Good. Come back and tell me how you get on, won't you?"[1]

Part II looks at the three types of conversations we briefly referred to in Chapter 2, namely, conversations to develop people, conversations to build relationships, and conversations to make and review decisions. These three types of conversations are the essence of what we are trying to promote: meaningful conversations.

First up, we look at five conversations to develop people. The next chapter (Chapter 6) suggests five more development conversations.

All good leaders instinctively know that developing people is their primary leadership responsibility. They also spend more time than most having development conversations with their key people. They do this because they know that the time invested is well worthwhile. Other managers will make the excuse that they don't have the time. Which is code for: "It is not a high priority for me to spend time conversing with my employees." If a leader has the view that their primary leadership role is developing people, then they also know that the best way to do this is through regular one-to-one conversations.

What are some of the conversations that are developmental? There are several frameworks around for this, but one you might like to consider is the Five Conversations Framework. This framework was developed as a substitute for the traditional performance review. Traditional performance reviews are not what we classify as developmental conversations; instead of performance development, performance reviews are essentially about performance assessment.

In a nutshell, the five conversations are:

1. Climate review conversation.
2. Strengths and talents conversation.
3. Opportunities for growth conversation.
4. Learning and development conversation.
5. Innovation and continuous improvement conversation.

For more detailed information on the Five Conversations Framework, look for the book: *The End of the Performance Review: A New Approach to Appraising Employee Performance.*[2] But in brief, let's consider this framework here as a means of having five sequential, developmental conversations with employees.

Climate review conversation

The climate review conversation is concerned with job satisfaction, morale, and communication. Although people's opinion about these matters can fluctuate over the course of a year, we think it is important to take a snapshot of where your team members are at occasionally. This assists managers in getting a handle on the current state of the organization. Information from these conversations can be a rich source of qualitative and quantitative data for planning purposes. It is an easy place to start having a developmental conversation with each of your employees.

What questions should be asked?

The questions asked by the manager will vary depending upon the organization, although they will probably not vary too much from the suggestions made below. But the questions asked should at the very least cover the topics of job satisfaction, employee morale, and communication.

As a guide here are some questions that cover these three areas:

- *On a scale of 1 to 10 (10 being high and 1 low), how would you rate your current job satisfaction?*

The response to this question ought to be followed by a supplementary qualitative question such as:

- *Why did you give it this rating?*

This question allows the employee to elaborate on their rating. For example, if someone gives it a 9, their response may be something like: "Because I believe we work well as a team and that gives me a lot of satisfaction personally." Or if they give it a 1, their response may be something like: "I don't feel I have the necessary resources or support to enjoy my job." Whatever the response, the manager has a rating and a reason for the rating. Job satisfaction ebbs and flows depending on a host of factors. This rating and the associated reason for it provide a benchmark for a follow-up climate review conversation later in the year.

The next question may be something like:

- *On a scale of 1 to 10 (10 being high and 1 low), how would you rate morale in the department/section/team you are working in?*

Morale, also known as *esprit de corps* when discussing the morale of a group, is a term used to describe the intangible capacity of people to maintain belief in an organization or a goal, or even in themselves and others. It refers to the level of individual faith in their team's capacity to contribute positively to organizational outputs. Why is this so important?

Workplace events such as heavy layoffs, the cancellation of overtime, a reduction in the number of benefits programs, and a lack of union representation play a large part in changing employee morale. Other events can also influence workplace morale, such as absenteeism through inappropriate sick leave by colleagues, low wages, and employees being mistreated. These kinds of things can adversely affect performance but can sometimes be dealt with by the manager and their colleagues.

As with the first question, the supplementary question would be:

- *Why did you give it this rating?*

This provides some justification for the rating and the issue or issues influencing the rating. For example, if an employee gives morale a 9 out of 10, they may follow up by saying something like: "People in our team work together to get the job done, no matter what is in front of them." On the other hand, someone may give it a 1 and follow up with a comment like: "Some people in our team are just not pulling their weight and that affects those that are." Once again the individual and collective results serve as a useful benchmark for a second conversation later in the year.

In terms of communication, a good starting question would be:

- *On a scale of 1 to 10 (10 being high and 1 low), how would you rate communication within our team and outside our team?*

We realize that the term *communication* can and does mean many things. The recipient of the question can and should interpret it however they want. Although the question can be interpreted differently by each person, it does invite the employee to understand communication however they like. This is not a bad thing at all. It allows the employee to say what is on their mind in relation to the concept of communication. And in so doing, it provides the manager with some focus on what their team consider at that particular time and in that particular space to be important.

For instance, an employee may consider communication in the context of their relationship with their manager. Or it could be interpreted as communication within their team, across the organization, or with customers and external stakeholders. The question is purposely designed to be open-ended so as not to constrain respondents' thinking on the concept of communication. And in being so, it sheds light on the communication issues that are important to employees at the time of the conversation and how they evaluate this perspective on communication at the time of the conversation.

As with the two previous questions, the added question of *why* invites the employee to state the reason for their rating:

• *Why did you give it this rating?*

A manager may get several different ratings from this question. One rating may be concerned with communication within the employee's team and another rating may concern the flow of information from and to the team. For instance, if someone has given communication 9 out of 10, they may say something like: "Our meetings are short, sharp, and to the point." However, another person who has given it 9 may have an entirely different reason for their score, such as: "Senior management go to great lengths to explain the reason for their decisions and how they will affect us in our team." On the other hand, if someone has given it a 1, they may say something like: "We never get told anything and always find out at the last moment." Or: "I feel left out of the conversation at our staff meetings." Both responses are entirely different but nevertheless valid for that particular person and their unique perspective on communication.

These questions should be followed by another open-ended question:

• *Is there anything else you would like to comment on, regarding job satisfaction, morale, or communication?*

This invites the employee to feel comfortable adding anything else to the conversation and provides the manager with the opportunity to respond.

Strengths and talents conversation

Most performance discussions are fixated on what is going wrong; in other words, they focus on weaknesses and sometimes neglect to discuss particular strengths and talents. Tom Rath, in the #1 *Wall Street Journal* bestseller, *Strengths Finder 2.0* (2007), states:

> Society's relentless focus on people's shortcomings has turned into a global obsession. What's more, we have discovered that people have several times more potential for growth when they invest energy in developing their strengths instead of correcting their deficiencies.[3]

Apart from being a far more positive place to start discussing employee development, as Roth points out, building upon strengths has a higher payoff than working on overcoming weaknesses. This does not mean that we should not discuss deficiencies; we should, and that is why the framework's third conversation is about opportunities for growth. But starting with strengths makes perfect sense.

This conversation is not just about identifying strengths; it is also about how they may be deployed in the employee's current or future roles. Are there tasks and projects that may suit that particular person?

For instance, someone may have a talent for dealing with people but be stuck in an office looking at a computer screen all day. Perhaps the conversation may lead to more interface with customers. How can their job be restructured to allow more customer interface to occur? While learning about the strengths of employees may be an interesting exercise, it offers little benefit in isolation, unless the strengths can be better utilized in an employee's current and future organizational role.

What are the questions to ask?

Based on the three Ps concept – *P*eople practice what they *P*refer and ultimately become *P*roficient in it – a useful question to start the conversation on strengths and talents would be:

• *What are the tasks you enjoy doing most in your current job?*

Although employees should be given an opportunity to consider this question, managers may have to prompt them or give suggestions of what they think that person may enjoy most. The follow-up question is simple:

• *Why do you enjoy those sorts of tasks?*

This will provide the manager with more information on their employee's strengths. In response to the first question, they might say: "I enjoy liaising with customers." When asked why, they may respond with: "I enjoy people interaction." This would suggest that they have strengths in the general theme of promoting. The manager can discuss this further by asking:

• *In your current role, how can we work together to provide you with the opportunity to do more of this?*

Of course, there may not be a straightforward answer. For example, the employee may be an accounts clerk whose work is mostly dealing with figures. But on reflection – and after discussing this with the accounts clerk – the manager might recognize that this employee's talents are most suited to working with customers rather than doing the accounts. Although the manager may not be able to change this in the short term, they can start planning to reshape the employee's role in order to maximize their talents in the future.

A T   T H E   C O A L   F A C E . . .

Enthusiastic blogger

A blogger went online to provide his endorsement for the Five Conversations Framework. Here is what he had to say:

"I want to start by saying that I very much like the approach of the Five Conversations. It represents a systematic approach and [is] a useful tool for obtaining the information the team leaders, top management, and HR professionals need to know. I for one am interested in using this approach. My personal experience with annual job appraisals is more positive than most, although I know there's a whole spectrum of good and bad practice out there. I think the contribution they make is partly a question of management style: a good manager with an open, participative style will adapt and use the process in a constructive manner. A good manager should also be collecting the information that is targeted by the Five Conversations Framework and if his or her current communication channels do not facilitate this exchange then they will benefit in my view by adopting the Five Conversations approach."[4]

Opportunities for growth conversation

This conversation focuses on strategies for improved performance from the employee's individual perspective. It provides the team member with an opportunity to consider how they may improve their own work performance. From here, the pair can discuss some tangible ways and means of improving individual productivity. This conversation is important to reflect on the individual's organizational role and how to improve their contribution. Many of the strategies can be implemented on the spot with the assistance of the manager. Other ideas can be discussed and put into practice later.

What are the questions to ask?

A good starting question in the Opportunities for Growth conversation may be:

 • *If there is one area where you believe you have an opportunity for growth, what would it be?*

This question invites the employee to critically reflect on their own performance. Being an open-ended question, it is stated in such a way as to invite the possibility that the employee does not see any room for improvement in their current role. Of course, there is always room for improvement. But the question is designed in such a way that the manager is not immediately zeroing in on an area they are concerned about.

It is not necessarily going to be helpful, on the other hand, to say something like: "Now, I have a real concern about your inability to manage your time and priorities. What are you going to do about this?" This kind of statement and question – at the very least – invites the employee to be defensive and, at worst, creates hostility. Neither is helpful, regardless of how right the manager may be about this claim!

On the assumption that the employee has mentioned something worthy of further discussion, the follow-up question may be:

 • *Can you elaborate on this so that I understand what you mean?*

This is an invitation to the employee to explain in their own words what they mean. It is entirely possible that the person asking the question knows what the employee means, but this is not the point. The point is to fully and respectfully understand the employee's perspective on the performance matter and to get them to *own* the performance issue.

Here, it is tempting for the manager to say: "I agree!" if they do agree, or no "I don't agree" if they do not. By making this sort of statement, the manager has effectively closed off the possibility of discussing their employee's perspective any further.

In these situations, consider ABC as a way expressing a view. A stands for antecedent, B for behavior, and C for consequences. The manager ought to invite the employee to explain the behaviors (B) that they consider need improving. Let us imagine that the employee says the following: "I think I need to improve my computer skills" to the initial question: *If there is one area where you believe you have an opportunity for growth, what would it be?* On the invitation by the manager to elaborate, they then say, "I have trouble with Excel and I use it regularly in my work." When the manager understands their employee's perspective fully, they may ask: "Why do you have trouble with Excel?" (A). The employee may reply by saying they have not been given the opportunity to learn this skill formally. And finally, the manager may ask them: "How is this affecting your work?" (C). They may say that it takes twice as long to produce spreadsheets.

The next question, once the manager has fully understood their employee's perspective on the question *Can you elaborate on this so that I understand what you mean?* is:

• *What can we do to improve this performance?*

Notice that we use the term *we* in this question. The implication of using the term *we* is that the manager is prepared – wherever possible – to help the employee and support their growth. Ultimately, the manager wants their staff to take responsibility for their own growth. But the employee has an expectation that their manager will support them to do so, or at least not put roadblocks in the way.

We would suggest the manager tackles at least two issues of growth in this conversation. So, the next question could be:

• *Apart from that, what is another area in your current role that you think is an opportunity for growth?*

The manager then repeats the sequence of questions.

It is better to tackle two areas for growth thoroughly than several in a superficial manner. Of course, the manager can respectfully agree or disagree with their employee's perspective at any time. But the important point here is that, through a series of questions, the manager is assisting the employee to take a sense of ownership for their own growth and development.

If the manager feels that there are other areas of performance where the employee can improve, a statement like:

• *Can I suggest another area you might consider is ...*

is a good way to start.

From here, the manager ought to offer a couple of critical incidents that illustrate their point.

Then the manager should invite the employee to comment on the suggestion for improvement with questions like:

• *What's your opinion about this?*
• *What are behaviors you believe you are (not) doing that are leading to this incident?*

If the employee is on the same page as their manager, then it is a matter of guiding the employee to finding a way to lift their performance in this particular area.

On the other hand, if the employee does not agree with their manager's observation, then this disagreement needs to be discussed. In these cases, the manager needs to be firm but respectful. It is important for the manager to disagree and explain why. This can be done by explaining the expectations the manager has of their staff and where they think that particular employee is falling short. The manager should then ask the employee whether they are clear on their expectations and how they may work together to ensure that the employee meets those expectations in the future.

Learning and development conversation

Learning and development conversations are about how the manager and employee can develop innate talents and overcome weaknesses identified in the previous two conversations. This conversation is designed to discuss the learning needs of the employee now and in the future. It may include formal opportunities, such as attendance at courses, programs, and seminars, and informal opportunities like skill development within the organization, or further coaching and mentoring. These discussions are important to establish some short-term goals for personal and technical growth and career development.

This conversation also provides an opportunity for employees to discuss their careers in broader terms. Since the learning and development conversation is focused on the future, it opens up the possibility of how the organization can assist the individual to meet their broader career needs from a learning and development perspective.

Like the Strengths and Talents and the Opportunities for Growth conversations, the Learning and Development conversation can assist in succession planning and employee retention. Often employees leave an organization because they cannot envisage how the organization can assist them to fulfill their career goals. The manager can benefit from these conversations by aligning their perceptions with their team members' perceptions. Individuals benefit from these discussions by exploring career and development opportunities within and outside the organizational structure, and ways in which their manager can assist them in their current role.

What are the questions to ask?

Once again, the questions asked by the manager in this conversation will vary depending upon the industry and the nature of the job. Nevertheless, they should cover the dimensions of technical learning, personal development, and problem-based learning.

As a guide, here are some questions that cover these three areas:

For technical learning, a good introductory question could be:

- *How would you rate your technical skills on a scale of 1 to 10 (10 being high and 1 low)?*

To assist with the focus of this question the manager might run through the technical aspects of the employee's job. For most jobs, there are usually five to eight key result areas.

Supplementary questions may include:

- *What technical areas do you think you have mastered?*
- *What technical areas of your job could be improved?*
- *Why do you say that? Can you give me an example?*

These questions may have been explored in the previous two conversations on Strengths and Talents and Opportunities for Growth. The difference here is that we are looking at how to capitalize on strengths and, in particular, how to overcome deficiencies. So the conversation ought to inevitably move on to ways and means of building on these strengths and opportunities for growth through learning opportunities.

Aside from the technical aspects of the employee's job, the manager should consider their personal development.

In terms of personal development, a manager could ask:

- *What are some areas that you would like to develop in personally or explore further for your own growth to help you become even more effective and efficient in your work?*

Follow-up questions could be:

- *Why do you say that?*
- *Can you cite an example?*

In particular, it would be useful to draw on dimensions of their non-job roles, such as team role, career role, and innovation and continuous improvement role.[5]

For example, in terms of improving an employee's team role, a manager may consider such things as communication, understanding yourself and others you work with, and leadership.

For the career role, the manager ought to reflect on some of the points raised in the Strengths and Talents conversation. In other words: What learning would assist you in capitalizing on your strengths to further develop your career?

What learning would enhance the employee's ability to improve their own capacity to develop ways and means of adding value to their organizational role? The development of an employee's innovation and continuous improvement role could benefit from learning such as risk analysis, conducting audits, or research and report-writing skills.

For problem-based learning, here is an opening question for managers:

- *What problems or dilemmas have you had to deal with over the past few months that were challenging?*

We would be surprised and disappointed if an employee could not think of a situation or dilemma. That would suggest that either they are not being stretched enough in their current role or they have come to the conversation unprepared.

At any rate, the manager should invite them to elaborate on the issue. The key questions are:

- *What happened?*
- *How did you approach the situation?*

• *What did you learn from it?*
• *How would you do things differently next time?*

If appropriate – from a learning and development perspective – they may ask the employee:

• *What knowledge, skills, or capabilities would have helped you deal with this issue?*

Problem-based learning is often less formal and can be undertaken in-house. For instance, it might be a question of learning to implement a set of guidelines for dealing with similar dilemmas that are anticipated in the future. Or it could be a discussion of alternative courses of action in a crisis. Then again, it may be a matter of personal coaching or support from the manager or others the employee works with who have had similar dilemmas.

By asking the types of questions we have outlined above, managers are covering the three approaches to learning and development we discussed earlier in the chapter. Therefore the conversation about learning and development goes beyond the technical requirements of the employee's job.

Innovation and continuous improvement conversations

Innovation and continuous improvement conversations are about ways and means of improving systems and processes, and presenting ideas for improving productivity in the business. Conversations about innovation and continuous improvement are about practical ways and means of improving both the employee's own efficiency and effectiveness and those of the organization as a whole. They focus on ideas for developing new and improved working arrangements for the individual and the organization. It is likely that a conversation with your staff about this topic will lead to the immediate generation of some practical and cost-effective ideas that can be used to enhance systems and process improvements across the organization.

Some of these ideas can be implemented to improve the competitiveness of the organization and the way it conducts itself in society and the marketplace. In other words, outcomes arising from the conversation on innovation and continuous improvement can be used by management as an opportunity to evaluate and implement ideas both within the team and across the organization.

What are the questions to ask?

Here are some areas that may assist in focusing the Innovation and Continuous Improvement conversation:

- Improving quality.
- Reducing time.
- Reducing costs.
- Increasing output.
- Increasing safety.
- Meeting deadlines.
- Enhancing interpersonal cooperation.
- Streamlining systems and processes.

As a guide, here are some questions that cover continuous improvement and innovation.

A starter question might be:

- *Thinking about the job you do for us, what could you do to improve the quality of the product or service we provide?*

Follow-on questions could include:

- *How would you go about this?*
- *What support would you need from me and others?*

With regard to reducing time, you might ask:

- *Is there anything you can think of that would reduce the amount of time required to process your work and speed up implementation?*

Again, supplementary questions could be:

- *How would you go about this?*
- *What support would you need from me and others?*

With regard to reducing costs, you could ask:

- *What cost savings have you identified, if any?*

This could be followed by:

- *How would you go about this?*
- *What support would you need from me and others?*

For improvements in output, you could ask:

- *Is there any way that you could implement a system or process that increased output without increasing your time on the job?*

Follow up with:

- *How would you go about this?*
- *What support would you need from me and others?*

In terms of safety, you might ask:

- *Have you any ideas about ways and means of increasing on-the-job safety and improving on our current safety record?*

Follow up with:

- *How would you go about this?*
- *What support would you need from me and others?*

For improvement in meeting the deadlines of customers, you could ask:

- *How could we improve our record on meeting customer deadlines? Any ideas?*

Follow with:

- *How would you go about this?*
- *What support would you need from me and others?*

In terms of team cooperation, you might ask:

- *How would you go about improving the cooperation between teams? Do you have any suggestions?*

Supplementary questions could be:

- *How would you go about this?*
- *What support would you need from me and others?*

A conversation on improvements in systems and processes might start with the following questions:

- *What about our systems and processes? How could they be improved from your perspective?*

And follow with:

- *How would you go about this?*
- *What support would you need from me and others?*

Obviously, you can tailor these questions to the industry you are in. Some will be more relevant than others.

But by adopting this thorough approach you are guaranteed to get a lot more practical suggestions that could be implemented across the organization to improve the business than by simply asking: "Do you have any suggestions for improving things?" The opportunity to generate ideas largely depends upon the amount of thought put in by the people involved in this conversation. As with all the conversations, the organization ought to give people the opportunity to consider the subject before the conversation takes place.

Although each of these five conversations ought to be a separate discussion, there will most likely be overlaps and common themes. In summary, though, the process assists in determining the current organizational climate, auditing strengths and talents and assessing how they can be more effectively deployed, discussing opportunities for growth, identifying learning and development needs, and considering ways and means of enhancing individual and organizational innovation and continuous improvement. These are issues that ought to be discussed – but are sometimes overlooked – in the formal annual or bi-annual performance appraisal. By breaking these important performance issues into distinct areas for discussion, the new framework offers a sharper focus and a clearer structure for individual and organizational performance enhancement.

The **Top 10** Key Points...

1. In a nutshell, the five conversations in the framework are: climate review conversation; strengths and talents conversation; opportunities for growth conversation; learning and development conversation; and innovation and continuous improvement conversation.

2. The Five Conversations Framework was developed as a substitute for the traditional performance review. However, it is a useful framework for developmental conversations.

3. The climate review conversation is concerned with job satisfaction, morale, and communication.

4. The strengths and talents conversation is not just about identifying strengths; it is also about how they may be deployed in the employee's current or future roles.

5. The opportunities for growth conversation focuses on strategies for improved performance from the employee's individual perspective.

6. Learning and development conversations are about how the manager and employee can develop innate talents and overcome weaknesses identified in the previous two conversations.

7. Innovation and continuous improvement conversations are about ways and means of improving systems and processes, and presenting ideas for improving productivity in the business.

8. Although each of these five conversations ought to be a separate discussion, there will most likely be overlaps and common themes.

9. Employees ought to be given time to consider the questions in each of the five developmental conversations.

10. The framework assists in determining the current organizational climate, auditing strengths and talents and assessing how they can be more effectively deployed, discussing opportunities for growth, identifying learning and development needs, and considering ways and means of enhancing individual and organizational innovation and continuous improvement.

Development Conversations: Five More Conversations

In addition to the five performance conversations, opportunities abound for additional conversations that support, acknowledge, enable, and encourage the development of others.

A senior state public servant took on responsibility for a department with employees and offices across the state. His primary task upon taking up his new role was to regenerate a sense of purpose and value among the staff, who had for several years felt ignored and undervalued.

To do this he set his managers the responsibility of engaging more directly with their staff and with him to ensure issues were addressed and ideas were tapped. Most importantly, he made a priority of getting out and about, meeting not just the managers in different locations and not just holding formal briefings, but directly conversing with staff.

The result was a groundswell of support for him and a renewed energy across the department. It was interesting to note that the department's work had not changed, its budget had not improved, nor had it received any formal recognition from on-high. The staff had simply seen real, personalized, engaged conversations in action – and they responded with their input, concerns, and energy.

The Five Conversations Framework offers a practical guide to enabling ongoing and intentional conversations designed to support improving performance, rather than making performance conversations a "test" or formal assessment.

Conversations that focus on and are designed to support ongoing development are an important and valuable part of any individual's career, any organization's culture, and therefore any manager's responsibilities. The challenge, of course, is that managers have many responsibilities and typically report that they are struggling just to keep up with the urgent things they have to do and simply lack the time to get to important things like developmental conversations.

But what if the issue became urgent? For example, what happens when a key employee asks to see their manager and says, "It's been great working here, but I've had another offer and it offers a really good challenge that I think I need, so I'll be leaving." Boom! Suddenly that vaguely important developmental conversation becomes an urgent discussion about what it would take to keep them, then (because rarely does anyone change their mind) an urgent meeting with the HR department about recruiting someone new, then a round of urgent interviews, another round of urgent meetings to work out who to offer the position to, then a series of induction discussions, then the inevitable team meetings. How did we find all that time?

AT THE COAL FACE ...

The new recruit

One of the authors recalls speaking to an 18-year-old woman fresh out of school and nine months into her first job in an SME.

She was quite distressed. Melinda had not received any feedback from her boss in nine months on the job. The author asked Melinda whether she would like him to approach her manager on her behalf and ask him if he could let her know how she was settling into her first job. Melinda was quite enthusiastic about this prospect and the author subsequently approached her boss, Ted. He proceeded to explain to Ted that Melinda was concerned that she had not received any feedback from him since she had started and suggested that he sit her down and explain how she was doing in her work. Before the author could finish his sentence, Ted interrupted him and said, "No, I can't do that." There was an uncomfortable pause in our conversation.

The author said, "May I ask why you can't do this?" He was thinking there must be some rational explanation. Ted retorted, "If I do that for Melinda, I will have to do that for all my staff."

Once again, the author was rendered speechless.[1]

When we have no choice, we simply have to find the time and other things get pushed aside, ignored, delayed, or delegated. Life goes on. So what if, instead of waiting for a critical moment, we proactively scheduled time to engage in regular, developmentally focused conversations? Just like the Five Conversations Framework, regular formal and informal development conversations do not have to take a lot of time. But they are an investment – in the team member, in the relationship between the manager and the employee, in the company's talent, and in the productivity of the business unit.

In addition to the five regular and structured performance conversations, there are also five informal development conversations that can take place spontaneously and frequently as needed and as a manager sees the opportunity. These five developmental conversations are the:

1. Coaching conversation.
2. Mentoring conversation.
3. Delegating conversation.
4. Visioning conversation.
5. Encouraging conversation.

While each of these can of course be structured and formal conversations, we also suggest they be seen as part of the normal, everyday conversation of the workplace. Many may already be happening to some degree but without intent; the potential for these conversations is typically rich but untapped; the opportunities are present every day.

Coaching conversation

According to Tony Grant and Jane Greene, in *Solution Focused Coaching: Managing People in a Complex World*:

> Coaching is about creating positive directed change. It is about helping people to develop their potential. Managers can use coaching to enhance and increase the performance of individuals and teams.

They describe coaching as a:

> collaborative, solution-focused, result-orientated and systematic process in which the coach facilitates the enhancement of work

performance, life experience, self-directed learning and personal growth of individuals.[2]

That sounds like a lot to accomplish in a single conversation. But that's also partly the point – you can only achieve these things through intentional conversations. Conversations are built on trust, intent, and commitment, and apply the key skills of asking questions and listening carefully. Developmental conversations can be in the areas of skill, performance, capability, or career. And while coaching conversations are frequently and perhaps typically seen as scheduled, structured events, it's also true that developmental coaching conversations can take place informally, spontaneously, and briefly. We might call it "corridor coaching."

This unstructured corridor coaching can and should take place frequently in response to issues, challenges, questions, and opportunities that arise in the normal course of workplace interaction. The major shift for the coaching leader is a shift in mindset from telling to asking, as we pointed out in Chapter 4. An underpinning principle of coaching is that the coach is helping the person being coached to find their own answers, not simply dictating what to do. If that's all it required you could send an email. Developing others is about ensuring they take greater ownership and responsibility for actions and results. That's why the discipline of asking questions is so important; as is listening, which we cover in more detail in Part III.

The opportunities to engage intentionally and constructively with your team members and colleagues through quick, spontaneous coaching conversations occur every day. If you have the mindset to commit to their development by focusing on solutions, learning and positive change, asking good questions, listening attentively, and clarifying next steps, you can help turn a potential frustration into another step in someone's development.

Mentoring conversation

While coaching and mentoring are clearly related, and the descriptions sometimes used almost interchangeably, there is a difference in dialogue. Where the coaching conversation is solution-focused and driven by the needs and goals of the person being coached, the mentoring conversation is often more general in nature and tends to directly tap the experience and expertise of the mentor.

Mentoring happens indirectly through the observations people make about others – especially those in formal leadership positions – reminding us again that our day-to-day example is one of the most powerful conversations we have. Mentoring also happens informally through conversations we have with those we respect and admire, taking the opportunity to find out more about their views, their insights, and their wisdom. And mentoring happens formally through intentional relationships that we establish for the express purpose of learning more about our profession, about leadership, or about some related aspect of our development.

A T   T H E   C O A L   F A C E   ...

The origins of the word mentor

The word "mentor" comes to us from Homer's work, *The Odyssey*. When Odysseus embarked on the Trojan wars he entrusted the care of his son, Telemachus, to a wise and trusted advisor, named Mentor. The idea of younger people being mentored by trusted older and wiser persons is typical across societies and cultures.

More recently, a new form of mentoring has emerged too, as younger people help their elders understand and grasp new technologies.

Mentoring can operate at several "levels" and may shift between those levels as needs and relationships change. For example, a mentor directly trains, coaches, or equips the mentee in a specific skill, role, or professional quality. Another form of mentoring might see the mentor taking more of a role as a counsellor or sponsor who provides support and guidance as needed.

The potential opportunities for mentoring include when people are:

• Commencing or preparing for a new role.
• Transitioning into new responsibilities.
• Preparing to undertake responsibilities on a new project.
• Needing to debrief a critical incident.
• Seeking feedback and support for their development.

Being prepared for the mentoring conversation means firstly understanding the need others may have for mentoring (often best learned by being mentored yourself), and secondly acknowledging what you have to contribute as a mentor – being a trusted adviser.

Delegating conversation

One of the most apparently basic skills of effective management is delegation. And yet, our workshops consistently reveal it is one of the least used leadership capabilities. There are a number of reasons why we avoid or resist delegating, including: not having anyone able or confident enough to delegate to; not having the time to properly delegate a responsibility; not wanting to endure the hassle – "it's just easier if I do it myself."

There is a time to delegate, and a time not to delegate, but when someone is clearly demonstrating the ability to take ownership of a task it is frustrating for them and limiting of us not to delegate.

Of course, we know there are other reasons we don't delegate too: not wanting to delegate tasks that we really enjoy doing ourselves; not wanting our delegation to be perceived as dumping unwanted work on people; not being comfortable with delegating tasks and as a resulting losing control. But if we fail to delegate we fail to develop others and we fail to develop ourselves. In addition, the less we delegate the less time we have to engage in developmental conversations with those we lead.

The delegating conversation is not about dumping work or responsibility on someone else, nor is it about abrogating our own responsibilities. It's about incrementally increasing others' responsibility as part of their continuing development. Dan Pink has written and spoken about the three key motivators at work: *autonomy*, *mastery*, and *purpose*.[3] Each can be related back to delegation: when responsibility is delegated to me I experience greater autonomy in how I accomplish my work; when tasks are delegated to me, my mastery is acknowledged; when I accept the delegation I am more closely connected to the purpose of the work I am responsible for.

Because "role clarity" is such a frequent concern in organizational life (as evidenced by organizational survey results), the delegating conversation must be a clear conversation. What is being delegated, and what isn't? Who now has the delegation and who needs to know that to ensure it works? What are the expectations associated with the delegation in terms of reporting and accountability?

Because delegation doesn't have to mean delegating 100 per cent of the responsibility for a task or project, delegating conversations have the potential to be frequent and ongoing. You might choose to delegate one or two discrete aspects of the task – useful if you want to check out someone's readiness for additional responsibility; delegate the task but limit the authority – to ensure they don't run too far ahead of your control and accountability; delegate an initial stage such as brainstorming, options generation, or research – to generate fresh ideas and give learning opportunities. Other delegating conversations can occur around asking for suggestions about what you could/should delegate.

As much as we might worry about dumping work on others, many managers are seen as carrying too many responsibilities that others could pick up (and maybe even do better!). This type of conversation can easily be linked to discussions about team members' development and growth in their roles.

We often hear that delegating is too hard because it just takes too long to do. And there's no escaping the fact that delegation takes more time initially, because it requires preparation, education, and evaluation – in short, it requires a conversation. If conversations are at the heart of the contemporary manager's work, as we pointed out in Chapter 1, then the delegating conversation needs to be a regular part of their communication – not only as part of their team members' development, but as part of their own development too.

Visioning conversation

James Kouzes and Barry Posner gave us the five practices of exemplary leaders and included two that offer very direct developmental conversation opportunities: *Inspire a shared vision* and *Encourage the heart*.[4] Let's take the vision conversation first.

Vision can sound like a lofty concept, but it's actually a quite everyday need we have in our work and our lives. We all crave a sense of purpose and meaning in what we do. Simon Sinek reminds us in his book, *Start with Why: How Great Leaders Inspire Everyone to Take Action*, that "it doesn't matter what you do, it matters why you do it."[5] He explains that while most companies talk about "what" they do or make, and some can extol "how" they go about it, few can articulate the most powerful thing: "why" they do what they do. And it's the "why" that inspires.

As one of the authors mentions in his book, *The New Influencing Toolkit: Capabilities to Communicate with Influence*,[6] one of the core strategies for influencing is the generation of a compelling vision. Visioning communication is a way of answering the question: *Why* are we doing this task or project? For a leader, the *why* conversations are crucial to sharing the vision. *Why* what we do makes a difference, *why* what each person contributes is critical, *why* process is important, *why* accountability matters.

While it's easy to think of the vision conversation as something like a motivating half-time exhortation by a coach, it's worth thinking about what actually motivates us when we are conversing with our leaders. It's usually less about some grand strategy in which we're a small cog, than about their interest in our own contribution – particularly when we have a concern, complaint, or suggestion. Once again we're reminded that attention, listening, and empathy are key ingredients in any conversation and crucial to ensuring genuine dialogue in any relationship, team, or organization. This is a point that Kouzes and Posner make:

> As counterintuitive as it might seem, then, the best way to lead people into the future is to connect with them deeply in the present. The only visions that take hold are shared visions—and you will create them only when you listen very, very closely to others, appreciate their hopes, and attend to their needs. The best leaders are able to bring their people into the future because they engage in the oldest form of research: They observe the human condition.[7]

We look to organizational leaders for a sense of what the future holds – how strengths can be utilized, how weaknesses can be minimized or overcome, how threats will be dealt with, how opportunities will be realized, how we will remain viable and healthy. This "forward looking" quality is one of the key leadership traits Kouzes and Posner have identified people look for (in their research over 25 years).

Stories are another valuable but frequently ignored means of sharing the vision and value of what a team or organization is doing. Stories reach the heart, they tap into our visual memory and emotions, personalizing otherwise remote or abstract tasks. As far back as Aristotle, communicators have been advised to speak not only to the head but to the heart *(pathos)*. Rob Goffee, Professor of Organizational Behavior at London Business School, and Gareth Jones, former Director of Human Resources and Internal Communication at the BBC, remind us of our need for meaning and stories in organizational life in their book, *Why Should Anyone Be Led by You?*:

> The mistake many leaders make is to assume that followers can be engaged primarily through rational analysis and straightforward assertion of facts ... But this approach – on its own – is rarely successful in energising others ... In order to properly engage others, leaders need to construct a compelling narrative. They must find a way of looking at the world that allows others not only to understand their role in it but also to be excited by it.[8]

Looking for and sharing stories that illustrate the organization's vision and values in action is a powerful conversation and can be a valuable means of maintaining effective development conversations.

AT THE COAL FACE ...

The passionate young lawyer

A young law graduate with a passion for social justice and humanitarian care took a holiday job with World Vision, promoting child sponsorship and aid donations in shopping centers. It is hard, repetitive work that involves a lot of rejection, from averted eyes to outright refusal and occasional accusations of wasted money. Nevertheless, the young graduate's passion remained undimmed after months of this work. Why? Because the World Vision marketing team regularly and frequently gathered their team members to share experiences, celebrate successes, take input, and remind them of the purpose for the work they were doing. Their job is not simply about getting sponsorships but about maintaining World Vision's profile and using the opportunities for advocacy of the valuable work the organization does.

Encouraging conversation

There's an old saying that "no one cares how much you know until they know how much you care." And it reminds us that all the power and persuasive technique and even communication skill can still fail us if we neglect the very real power of emotion in the way we communicate with people.

Opportunities to engage in encouraging conversations are perhaps among the easiest (and certainly among the most pleasant) to identify in our working relationships. A key to bringing out the best in others is to express appreciation, acknowledge contributions, and celebrate achievements. Sincere individual recognition is a powerful motivator, feeding our need for significance. "Followers want to feel significant," say Goffee and Jones:

> In simple terms, they need recognition for their contribution. Social psychologists have made repeated pronouncements on this

profound human need for recognition. So it is remarkable how often as individuals we seem to want it but not give it.[9]

Perhaps it's a fear that our praise will be rejected that holds us back. Or maybe there's something in our psyche (or organizational culture) that says we need to be seen as "hard" rather than "soft." Whatever those misconceptions might be, if you want to encourage quality conversations then regular affirmation, recognition, and appreciation is going to have to be present. There's plenty of research that shows our human need for "positivity," and that maintaining a realistically positive perspective helps us be more creative and productive.

A T   T H E   S C R E E N   F A C E   …

Even recognition by email works …

When Rob took over a team dispersed across his state, his management style of regular face-to-face interactions to provide a constant flow of feedback, recognition, and appreciation was challenged by distance and separation. Telephoning people sometimes worked, but of course they weren't always available – and he worried about catching them at a bad time for what he considered important messages. So he reluctantly resorted to email on occasion. An early experience was hearing of a positive initiative taken by a remote employee. He drafted an email simply saying he'd been told about it and expressing his appreciation for the work that the person had done. He was later simultaneously pleased and concerned by what he heard about the person receiving his message. Pleased because they were so happy about it they printed it out and posted it at their desk, even pointing it out to colleagues who dropped by. Concerned because it was such a big deal – a completely new experience for the employee (and their colleagues) to receive a simple note of recognition and appreciation from their manager.

One of the simplest, most effective, and yet most neglected forms of encouragement can be expressed in two words: *thank you*. Thank you for showing such initiative; thank you for staying back late to complete that project; thank you for speaking up yesterday during the meeting and expressing your point-of-view; thank you for dealing with that customer so professionally under difficult circumstances. Like all useful feedback, if it is done in the right place, at the right time, in the right way, with the right intention, to the right person, it will be a source of encouragement.

One of the simplest, most effective, and yet most neglected way of encouragement can be expressed in two words: thank you.

Here is a simple and potent exercise to illustrate our point. For the next week, starting tomorrow, commit to having three brief conversations every day that are encouraging. If nothing else, it forces you to look for things that merit encouragement. Managers are very good at spotting situations in the workplace that are going wrong and feel a sense of obligation to point out these occurrences to employees. You can continue with this. It is part of your job as a leader. But try to balance it up with identifying three opportunities for having encouraging conversations. If you are not used to this approach, and genuine in your endeavor, you will be amazed at the impact of these conversations on morale, engagement, motivation, and general goodwill in your team.

This brings us to the end of the chapter. To supplement the Five Conversations Framework, we have provided you with another framework for developmental conversations. While the Five Conversations Framework ought to be a regular and structured series of developmental conversations, we have introduced you to five additional informal conversations that can take place spontaneously and frequently.

The coaching conversation can be used in the areas of skill development, performance improvement, capacity building, or career enhancement. Conversations that involve mentoring are less solution-focused and more driven by the needs of the person being coached. Mentoring conversations are more general in content and draw on the knowledge and skill of the mentor. The delegation conversation in essence is about gradually increasing the responsibilities of employees and their development. Conversations on visioning are based on discussing the *why* of work. (Dave and Wendy Ulrich wrote an interesting book with that title, *The Why of Work*.[10]) Visioning is about stepping back momentarily and reflecting on the link between our work and the vision of the organization. And finally, the encouraging conversation taps into our fundamental human need to feel significant. These conversations, while drawing on the tasks people do, are primarily about developing people.

The **Top 10** Key Points …

1. Conversations that focus on, and are designed to support, ongoing development are an important and valuable part of any individual's career, any organization's culture, and therefore any manager's responsibilities.

2. The five additional development conversations are: the coaching conversation; the mentoring conversation; the delegation conversation; the visioning conversation; and the encouraging conversation.

3 While each of these five additional conversations can be seen as part of the normal, everyday conversation of the workplace, they can also be engaged in more intentionally and frequently, for greater impact.

4 The coaching conversation can be in the areas of skill, performance, capability, or career.

5 Unstructured corridor coaching can and should take place frequently in response to issues, challenges, questions, and opportunities that arise in the normal course of workplace interaction.

6 Where the coaching conversation is solution-focused and driven by the needs and goals of the person being coached, the mentoring conversation is often more general in nature and tends to directly tap the experience and expertise of the mentor.

7 The delegating conversation is not about dumping work or responsibility on someone else, nor is it about abrogating our own responsibilities. It's about incrementally increasing others' responsibility as part of their continuing development.

8 Because delegation doesn't have to mean delegating 100 per cent of the responsibility for a task or project, delegating conversations have the potential to be frequent and ongoing.

9 While it's easy to think of the vision conversation as something like a motivating half-time exhortation by a coach, it's more about a leader's interest in their team member's contribution – particularly when they have a concern, complaint, or suggestion.

10 Opportunities to engage in encouraging conversations are among the easiest to identify in our working relationships. A key to bringing out the best in others is to express appreciation, acknowledge contributions, and celebrate achievements.

chapter 1

Conversations for
Building Relationships

Every conversation we have influences – and is influenced by – the relationship that exists between those in conversation. So it's important to plan, manage, and observe what's happening in conversations – our own and others'.

Can you imagine a situation where two people sat side-by-side in the workplace for ten years without uttering one word to each other; not even a hello, good morning, how are you? Not one word! Well, it happened.

One of the authors remembers working with an internationally recognized orchestra. Two musicians, who sit side-by-side on the stage and in rehearsal, refused to speak to one another for a decade. When they had to communicate with each other about artistic matters, they would write notes and pass them to each other, without making so much as eye contact.

After sitting down with each of the musicians in a one-on-one coaching session, the author was told of a relatively minor incident that occurred between the two artists early in their career in that particular orchestra. A violation of trust resulted from that encounter and they both decided not to speak to each other for what amounted to thousands of rehearsals, orchestral meetings, and concerts. It created tension in the section and ultimately across the orchestra. The section principal musician didn't know what to do, and ultimately gave up trying to reconcile their differences.

The author suggested both musicians meet together over coffee and talk to each other without anyone else present. The author arranged the meeting. And they did finally, reluctantly meet. Their differences were ironed out and now they are happily communicating again.

A frequent workshop discussion for us involves the issue of feedback. And it's interesting how most people acknowledge that when they hear the word "feedback" they instinctively tend to expect criticism – even though praise, acknowledgment, and recognition are also all forms of feedback. So the discussion often moves to looking for opportunities to communicate those things – partly in order to reset the tendency to assume feedback is inevitably critical or negative.

One line that we've found helps people to grasp the significance of sharing positive feedback is this: "If the only time I hear from you is when you think I've screwed up, what do you think that relationship is going to be like?"

It's not hard to imagine the quality of the relationship if the only feedback an employee receives from their manager is negative. My relationship with a manager who is constantly negative is likely to be one of avoiding interaction, taking no risks, being prepared to defend myself, and to see my manager as a threat rather than a supporter. From the manager's perspective, their relationship with me will be increasingly shaped by experiences of my defensiveness and lack of initiative. Neither of us is likely to be looking forward to our next interaction. Neither of us is likely to be sharing positive messages about the other with our extended networks. Neither of us is likely to be experiencing a sense of teamwork. Hardly surprising, since the experience each of us has of our conversations is characterized by criticism, defensiveness, authority, resistance, frustration, and resentment. Negative feedback, with no positive feedback, erodes the working relationship.

Consider how the dynamic might change. As my manager, supervisor, director, or colleague, you took the initiative to express appreciation for something I've done. Perhaps you shared a positive comment someone else had made about my work (or our team's work). Or you took a few minutes to ask how things were going? If the working relationship hasn't been great then it will take more than one interaction to recalibrate it, but it's a constructive starting point. And all it takes is a few of those types of genuine conversations to begin to reset the connections between us.

So let's look at some of the dynamics at play in conversations. At the same time, let's consider some of the principles and practices we can employ to use our conversations as opportunities to build healthier relationships that enable more robust and honest conversations.

Relationships, tasks, and processes

First, it's important to note that, naturally enough, most of our workplace conversations tend to be "task" focused, as we have discussed throughout the book. We're talking about goals, projects, processes, plans, actions, responses, and results. And that's appropriate, because teams need to be able to perform, achieve, and deliver. The danger, however, is that we miss the fact that the successful and sustainable performance of those tasks is directly affected by the relationships between those working on the tasks. Indeed, conflict in teams is typically summarized as occurring over task issues, relationship issues, or process issues – including the processes used to resolve task and relationship issues.

An analysis of 45 independent studies of team conflict (involving more than 3000 teams) found that: "conflict processes, that is, how teams *interact regarding* their differences, are at least as important as conflict states, that is, the *source* and *intensity* of those perceived differences."[1] Perhaps unsurprisingly, DeChurch, Mesmer-Magnus, and Doty found that what they called "collectivist processes" (such as openness and collaboration) produced better team outcomes than "individualistic processes" (such as competing or avoiding).[2] What seems like commonsense, though, is challenging – because individuals and teams often simply do not know how to engage in open and collaborative processes, especially in the midst of conflict.

What this suggests is that an intentional focus on conversations that build relationships is not an end in itself. Rather it is a practical means to ensuring that teams not only focus on and achieve their tasks, but also support the relationships within the team that enable tasks to be managed and achieved in cooperative, creative, and sustainable ways.

Which brings us back to the central role of conversations – the conversations individuals have with each other and the conversations teams have – and the principles and practices that underpin, shape, and empower those conversations. Let's look at some of these principles.

Trust

There's no doubting the central role of trust in relationships – whether we are talking relationships between people, between individuals and their leaders, or between people and their organizations.

Edelman PR have been tracking trust in government and business around the world for many years, each year releasing a "trust barometer." "We believe trust is an asset that enterprises must understand and properly manage in order to be successful in today's complex operating environment. Unlike reputation, which is based on an aggregate of past experiences with a company or brand, trust is a forward facing metric of stakeholder expectation."[3]

In his book, *The Speed of Trust*, Stephen M. R. Covey makes the case for investing in trust relationships with his equation that when trust goes up, speed goes up and cost goes down, and when trust goes down, speed goes down and cost goes up.[4] Or, as Ralph Waldo Emerson put it: "Our distrust is very expensive." In other words, trust or distrust is something that delivers or hinders individual, team, and organizational performance.

So how do we build trust? In short, the answer is: one conversation at a time.

There are numerous descriptions of trust, but some of the commonly agreed elements of trust are: openness, acceptance, congruence (alignment between what we say and what we mean), reliability, and competence. All of these are experienced, communicated, and assessed through conversations – both those we are a part of and those we observe. So let's take a quick surf through these five elements of trust in relation to conversations.

The level of appropriate openness we offer others in conversations gives others a sense of both our self-confidence and our willingness to connect with them. We talk about some people being "closed books" or "playing their cards close to their chest" – suggesting it's hard for us to know what they are really like. Trust requires a degree of openness or self-disclosure about ourselves. Yes, there's an element of risk – but trust is about creating safety and understanding so we can accomplish more together in the face of risk. Some people are more naturally open about themselves than others (which is not always a good thing – especially if you're seated next to them on a long flight!), but any relationship requires a commitment to sharing information and being appropriately self-disclosing in order to communicate a commitment to the relationship. We can't expect others to share information with us or let us know about themselves if we aren't willing to do the same. As leaders that means taking the first step in being open.

We can't expect others to share information with us or let us know about themselves if we aren't willing to do the same. As leaders that means taking the first step in being open.

Acceptance is the flipside of the openness coin. When people do share information about themselves they've chosen to take a risk, to be a little bit vulnerable. We all know there's the chance of rejection or judgment, so it's important that we are able to manage our prejudices and biases in order to accept others for who they are and accept their perspectives as their own – even if we don't agree.

Congruence in our communication is measured by how aligned our words are with what we mean. Do we talk straight or do we couch our opinions and contributions in qualifications or hesitant phrases? There's a balance here, of course, between bluntness and avoidance. We often trust blunt people a lot more than those who always try to make things "nice" by avoiding the hard issues. But bluntness also has its own limitations because often the language people use is a lot stronger than the actions they are prepared to take. Congruence is about assertiveness – that balance between aggressiveness and avoidance. It's an important element of trust because it communicates respect – respect for our own views and respect for the capacity of others to handle directness.

Reliability is perhaps the most familiar element of trust because at its base it sends a message about whether you will "do what you say you will do." Over-promising, under-delivering, procrastinating, and inconsistency quickly become associated with a lack of reliability – and erosion of trust.

Competence is a fifth element of trust – often associated with reliability – that is sometimes overlooked. We all learn to trust ourselves and others in some situations but not others. We may trust our own judgment in financial matters based on our expertise in that area, but not trust ourselves about a strategic decision because we acknowledge our limitations there. Likewise, we may trust our manager to competently organize a project but not to make a presentation about it to stakeholders. It depends on their task competence. Because our physical, emotional, and professional safety is fundamental to us, we instinctively look for demonstrated competence as a part of our trust assessment.

Each of these five elements of trust – openness, acceptance, congruence, reliability, and competence – are part of the conversations we have that build relationships. And it's important to be able to consciously incorporate them into our conversations.

A T   T H E   C O A L   F A C E ...

Growing trust in your work relationships

Nan Russell writes about trust as "the new workplace currency." In a 2013 *Psychology Today* article she suggests ten ways for growing trusting relationships:

"Relationships that enable trust and bring exceptional results don't happen unless there's a conscious intention to make them happen. That intention starts with common-sense approaches around *basic* relationship building. Below are ten ways to demonstrate that a work relationship matters.

Trust grows in relationships when ...

The relationships are mutually beneficial
You bring the best of who you are into the relationship; the best includes core elements like integrity, tolerance, honesty, and trustworthiness

You want the best for the other person

The relationship is more important than any single outcome

You invest time, communication, commitment, and authenticity

You show genuine care, concern, and compassion

You operate with appreciation, politeness, and inclusion

You give more than you take, while still keeping your interests in view

You help others achieve their aspirations, dreams, goals, or personal best

You respect where others are coming from – knowledge, experience, state of mind, values, beliefs, needs

Trust may be at historic lows, but so what? Trust is a local issue. If you want more trust in your work relationships, start with yourself. A practice of trust building is a practice of relationship building. If you want to grow trust or rebuild broken trust, focus on building your relationships."[5]

Recognition, appreciation, interest

Elsewhere in this book we look at the important but often neglected potential of positive conversations – conversations that focus on what's working well, what we appreciate, what we are grateful for. Such conversations are a natural means of expressing openness and acceptance as part of the trust building process. They are also energizing for both the recipient and the person delivering the positive messages.

One of the authors still recalls a wise summer camp director's mantra to his staff that every teenage camper should receive "a measure of challenge, a measure of achievement, and a measure of recognition every day." It's a practical aspiration that reminds us of the importance of respecting those we have the privilege of leading.

Goffee and Jones call it the need for "significance":

> Followers need to feel significant. In simple terms, they need recognition for their contribution. Social psychologists have made repeated pronouncements on this profound human need for recognition. So it is remarkable how often as individuals we seem to want it but not give it.[6]

Showing interest in others, expressing appreciation for efforts, and giving recognition for achievements and contributions are simple but powerful conversations that invest in relationships, building confidence and trust. We covered these ideas in Chapter 6.

Empathetic listening

"The ability and willingness to listen with empathy is often what sets a leader apart," says Christine Riordan, Provost and Professor of Management at the University of Kentucky. "Hearing words is not adequate; the leader truly needs to work at understanding the position and perspective of the others involved in the conversation."[7] Riordan urges leaders to focus on three skills to increase empathetic listening: observing nonverbal, processing information attentively and checking for understanding, and encouraging the conversation to continue through verbal and nonverbal acknowledgments. It reminds us that listening is not simply a transaction or exchange of words, but a relational connection that involves and affects the mind, the body, and the heart. And it's the heart aspect – the *pathos* – that human beings naturally remember most powerfully. Remember that old saying that "no one cares how much you know until they know how much you care."

A T   T H E   S C R E E N   F A C E...

Use conversations to start virtual team meetings

Writing in *Harvard Business Review*, author and consultant, Keith Ferrazzi, makes the following recommendation about using relationship-building principles as part of managing virtual team meetings.

"While employees who are in the same office commonly chat about their lives, virtual teammates do so much more rarely. Try taking five minutes at the beginning of conference calls for everyone to share a recent professional success or some personal news. This is probably the easiest way to overcome the isolation that can creep in when people don't work together physically."[8]

Four steps to relationship-building conversations

There's a lot going on in conversations. It's not just the words being spoken and heard. It's not even just the nonverbal communication – or absence of it – accompanying the conversation. It's more, even, than the interpretation of the message. It's the combination of all of these components and more that creates the relationship between conversation partners. So one way to think about effectively managing our conversations is through four practices that should be present in any relationship building conversation:

• Show up.
• Listen up.

- Speak up.
- Lift up.

Show up

Showing up is first and foremost about being present in the conversation. This may sound easy, but we all know how it feels when the person we are trying to communicate with is checking their phone or looking over our shoulder, or just has that slightly glazed look that silently but powerfully says, "Are you done yet?" Managing our attention is one of the hardest things we have to do in our busy, distracted lives. But since we can't be anywhere other than where we are, it makes sense to show up 100 per cent. We'll get more out of it, and our partners in conversation will contribute more knowing we are fully engaged.

In Chapter 1, we identified one of the paradoxes of leadership conversations as being in the moment and simultaneously having peripheral vision. Without peripheral vision, the conversation cannot be put into context. Leaders need the capacity to listen at two levels. At one level they need to be in the moment, and at another level they need to take into account a range of external factors affecting the current conversation. But there is a difference between maintaining these two levels of listening and showing up. Typing out an email while listening to an employee is not peripheral vision. It is often justified as "multitasking." Showing up means giving the other person your full attention.

Dr Adam Fraser contends that one of the great challenges we face is the task of dealing with the constant "transitions" between the many tasks and settings we work in every day:

> The key to business success is the ability to leave the mindset and baggage of the previous interaction behind and psychologically "show up" to the next one with a mindset that will get the most out of it.[9]

One of his practical tips is to anticipate the new interaction and ask ourselves how we want to show up – and then behave in that way. Without consciously redirecting our behaviors, our attention, and our thinking there's every likelihood we will behave in inappropriate and ineffective ways. How we show up is how people experience us. So, how do you want to show up? How do others need you to show up? How will the way you show up enrich the conversation and the relationship?

Listen up

Listening up we've already looked at, but it bears repeating that listening is foundational to our effectiveness as communicators, leaders, and influencers. And it's a key to the idea of "showing up" and being fully present. "The biggest mistake you can make in trying to talk convincingly is to put your highest priority on expressing your ideas and feelings," wrote John Maxwell in *Developing the Leader Within You*. "What most people really want is to be listened to, respected and understood. The moment people see that they are being understood they become motivated to understand your point of view."[10]

The challenges of really listening are many. Not least the fact that our brain's capacity to process information runs about four times the rate at which people speak. And it's further compounded by our tendency to assume we know where people are going with their thoughts rather than actually focusing on and processing what they're saying. This means we can easily find ourselves listening more actively to our own thoughts and judgments about the other person than to what they are actually saying. For many of us these two practical challenges are supplemented by the inability to focus – because we suffer with "monkey mind." Monkey mind is a term from Buddhism that describes the untrained mind as being restless and easily distracted, jumping chaotically from one idea to another, like a monkey in a tree. It's the internal dialogue that mentally interrupts, distracts, and distorts the moments and conversations we are actually in.

For more on practical listening skills, see Part III, Chapter 10.

Speak up

Speaking up may seem an obvious component in healthy conversations but everyone knows the frustration, uncertainty, and anxiety that is created when important issues are left unspoken. We talk about not talking about "the elephant in the room." Lots of words are said, but no one has the courage to speak up about what really matters. But when someone does display the courage and skill to speak up candidly, respectfully, and confidently about the real issue, everyone sits up straighter and recognizes that something important has happened. Leadership is happening.

That is a premise of the bestselling *Crucial Conversations*, by Patterson, Grenny, McMillan, and Switzler:

> Our research has shown that strong relationships, careers, organizations, and communities all draw from the same source of power – the ability to talk openly about high-stakes, emotional, controversial topics.[11]

The ability to speak up in those highly-charged situations doesn't happen spontaneously or accidentally. It is borne out of the experience of speaking up honestly, clearly, and respectfully in lots of everyday, ordinary conversations.

Showing up, listening up, and speaking up are all essential components in relationship-building conversations. But there's one additional element that we frequently overlook although it is often well within our reach – and it's one that can put your conversations on relationship steroids.

Lift up

Lifting up is the conscious commitment to leave the conversation with people feeling positive. Which sounds like a great idea, but ... what about when you have no choice but to criticize, correct, or insist on compliance? What about when the exchange has been terse, tough or filled with tension? Perhaps in such instances it's even more important to aim to "lift up" not just the other person but yourself and your shared conversation.

How? Definitely not with the old "feedback sandwich" (positive opening ... critical message ... positive close) – we all know to listen for that middle bit and ignore the rest. We can, however, keep a couple of principles in mind that can help ensure even those difficult conversations conclude on an upward note: conversation spirals, clear commitments, and affirmation.

You've probably noted the tendency for conversations to follow one of two directions: up or down. This is sometimes called the "upward spiral" or "downward spiral" of a conversation. In a downward spiral you hear the language and tone becoming negative, strained, tired, and de-energized; in upward spiral conversations, the language and tone maintain or even build energy through positive framing of messages, solution-focused debate, respectful listening, and a sense of shared purpose. As a leader and skilled communicator, it's important to be able to see and hear this spiral – directing the spiral up and intervening if it heads down.

Of course, some conversations will start heading down naturally as you get into the detail of a difficult issue. That's fine, but if you're going to work towards a solution and tap into positive mindsets, there's a point at which the downward problem focus needs to be transitioned into a future, solution focus. This is the idea of creating "shared meaning" and "co-creating" our conversations. Keeping a clear focus on what the issue is and what we're trying to achieve gives a strong impetus to maintaining an upward spiral.

This process is shaped right from our first words. The principle of "primacy and recency effect" suggests that the beginning and ending of a conversation will tend to have a heavier weighting on our recollection of our experience of conversations than the actual content. This reminds us again that "how we show up" (see "showing up" above) sets the tone and likely direction of a conversation, and that how we close will leave a lasting impression of the time and effort we've invested in the conversation. So ensuring that our conversations conclude with clear commitments – to action, to next steps, to further conversation – is important to leaving our conversation partner (and ourselves) with a sense of value, purpose, and progress from the interaction.

Clear commitments can include shared decision-making, clear direction, succinct summaries, or explicit next steps. It's easy for two people to leave the same conversation with different conclusions. So clarifying and confirming our shared understanding and commitments helps us maintain the positive energy in the conversation and the relationship.

Having maintained an upward spiral and concluded with clear commitments, we are in a good position to add one final touch – affirmation. Even when you have agreed to disagree, or simply confirmed that you have competing commitments, there's nothing (apart from overactive emotions) that prevents you from acknowledging the other party's contribution to the conversation. Saying "thank you," acknowledging particular contributions or perspectives, or expressing appreciation for their candor leaves the other person feeling respected and appreciated. As we mentioned in Chapter 6, it's a simple act but one that can make a powerful contribution to the working relationship as well as to how the issue is managed.

Relationship checkup

As a closing thought on conversations that build relationships, think about a significant relationship (whether professional or personal) where you may have cause for concern about the quality of your conversations. Take a moment to assess it on the following scales:

How appropriately do you typically "show up" for your conversations?

Not well at all									Very well
1	2	3	4	5	6	7	8	9	10

How well do you "listen up"?

Not well at all									Very well
1	2	3	4	5	6	7	8	9	10

How appropriately, respectfully, and confidently do you "speak up"?

Not well at all									Very well
1	2	3	4	5	6	7	8	9	10

How "lifted up" do you leave the conversation, the other person, and yourself?

Not well at all									Very well
1	2	3	4	5	6	7	8	9	10

Is the relationship currently getting

Weaker									Stronger
1	2	3	4	5	6	7	8	9	10

Is your satisfaction with the conversations within the relationship

Decreasing									Increasing
1	2	3	4	5	6	7	8	9	10

Are your conversations more typically

Accidental / Ad hoc / Reactive									Intentional
1	2	3	4	5	6	7	8	9	10

Do your conversations more typically spiral

Downwards									Upwards
1	2	3	4	5	6	7	8	9	10

In this chapter, we have covered some of the key principles in building relationships. We have looked at trust, recognition, appreciation, interest, and empathetic listening, and the four steps to relationship-building conversations. They include showing up, listening up, speaking up, and lifting up. We ended this chapter by providing you with an opportunity to evaluate a relationship and the kind of conversations you have had with that person, based on the four steps of relationship building.

The **Top 10** Key Points …

1. Successful and sustainable performance of tasks in the workplace are directly affected by the relationships between those working on the tasks.

2. There's no doubting the central role of trust in relationships – whether we are talking relationships between people, between individuals and their leaders, or between people and their organizations.

3 Elsewhere in this book, we look at the important but often neglected potential of positive conversations – conversations that focus on what's working well, what we appreciate, what we are grateful for.

4 Showing interest in others, expressing appreciation for efforts, and giving recognition for achievements and contributions are simple but powerful conversations that invest in relationships, building confidence and trust.

5 Listening is not simply a transaction or exchange of words, but a relational connection that involves and affects the mind, the body, and the heart.

6 The four practices that should be present in any relationship-building conversation are show up, listen up, speak up, and lift up.

7 Showing up is first and foremost about being present in the conversation.

8 Listening up is foundational to our effectiveness as communicators, leaders, and influencers.

9 Speaking up may seem an obvious component in healthy conversations but everyone knows the frustration, uncertainty, and anxiety that is created when important issues are left unspoken.

10 Lifting up is the conscious commitment to leave the conversation with people feeling positive.

8

Conversations for Making and Reviewing Decisions

Leaders get criticized for involving others too much or too little in the decision-making process; it is often hard to strike the right balance.

Sometimes leaders will be criticized for making decisions without consultation or collaboration and sometimes they'll get criticized for being too consultative and collaborative. It is more often than not a fine balancing act.

One of the authors remembers attending a meeting chaired by a manager of a well-known international orchestra. The orchestra manager was meeting with the section leaders of the orchestra. This manager was sometimes accused by others around the office of being too collaborative in his decision-making style, and this meeting was one such occasion!

At the meeting, the orchestra manager decided to raise the issue of one of the leading musicians in the orchestra's claim for leave to work with another orchestra. This orchestra manager wanted to work together with the leaders of the orchestra. He asked them what they thought of the idea of this musician (who was not present at the meeting) taking six weeks' leave to play in another orchestra.

One of the leading musicians in the meeting asserted: "That's your decision. We don't need you to check with us about leave. That's a managerial issue. You need to make that decision."

Let's cut to the chase: when communicating about decisions that need to be made, the majority of managers do this less as a dialogue and more as a monologue. Taking action and making decisions typically involves a manager briefing team members so they will dutifully (sometimes!) go off and carry out what is really a request; there is often little or no room for two-way interaction. A top-down request is not a conversation, it's a command. And then, after the instruction is carried out, a review of the job done by the employee is generally done in silence in the mind of the manager, if at all. More often than not, an after job review is not discussed openly. In the mind of the employee who has done the task, no debrief means: "no news is good news." But, if an employee hears from the manager, it is usually because something was not done satisfactorily. For many managers, with time impositions, a genuine decision-making conversation and review of the action taken – or not taken – may not seem a priority.

As we've said several times, real dialogue about work is often bypassed for other pressing matters. But conversations around complex decisions in particular, and post-action reviews or debriefs, can be hugely beneficial for a host of reasons. For instance:

- Conversation can ensure an alignment of expectations.
- Conversation can be crucial for clarifying and understanding the detailed requirements of a task or project.
- Conversation can be beneficial for sharing and exchanging ideas on a best way forward.
- Conversation can improve the decision-making process by bringing more than one perspective to the table.
- A better quality solution to a problem can result from a collaborative conversation.

A conversation can save time in the long run. So it is perplexing that investing some purposeful time conversing at the start and end of a task is not always a priority for managers.

Don't get us wrong; we are not suggesting that all decisions require a conversation before and after action is taken. Some decisions of course can and should just be made, without consultation or collaboration. But some decisions will undoubtedly benefit from interaction and dialogue with people within and outside an organization. In the mistaken belief that not discussing a course of action will save time, managers more often than not dive straight in and make a unilateral decision. But even when this is done with the best of intentions, after the action has been taken (or not taken correctly), managers often come to the realization that the lack of engagement at the outset has proved costly as they frustratingly have to spend extra time "picking up the pieces." Inappropriate execution or lack of action may well be due to a misunderstanding, false assumptions, or lack of clarity; all potentially resolved through a briefing conversation.

Managerial decision-making involving others can be classified in the following three ways:

1. Decisions requiring consultation and input from others.
2. Decisions made collaboratively with others.
3. Decisions made by others with some input from the manager.

Generally speaking, one of these three decision-making approaches involving others probably feels more comfortable and suits your style. Our natural decision-making preference can result in us exercising one of these three approaches too frequently, regardless of the circumstances. Although we all understand the intrinsic value of each approach to decision-making, our predisposition for one may negatively skew its use. We may be prone to using this preferred approach too often and consequently at the wrong time and place. Exercising each of the three approaches in the right place, at the right time, and with the right people enhances our decision-making capability.

All leaders, regardless of their experience, develop their own decision-making style; and so they feel more comfortable in one of these three domains. What's more, we all find it fairly easy to justify or rationalize our favored approach. Conversely, one of the other three approaches can feel less comfortable to execute; it is incongruent with our preferred leadership style. This uneasiness can result in avoidance of a warranted and appropriate approach. Other factors also come into play when we choose a decision-making approach. But our personal preference, organizational conditioning, and comfort zone can't be ignored.

To better manage our natural preferences, the context surrounding the decision ought to shape our choice. Is this the kind of decision that requires input from others? Do I need to seek out other people's opinions about this decision? Do we as a team need to be united and committed to a particular course of action? Are there questions we need to consider? In a dilemma facing the team, is it best for me to act as a "sounding board" or offer a solution? These are some of the issues we grapple with. Our preferred style, and the circumstances we face, to a large extent shape the kind of interaction we have with others when making decisions.

Beyond the situation we face and our personal preferences, a third important dimension affects our approach to decision-making: the people affected by the decision. Some questions related to the people dimension are: How much expertise and skill does the individual or team have in relation to the situation? Alternatively, how much knowledge and understanding do I have about this situation? What are the expectations others hold about their involvement in this matter? How much of a priority is this decision likely to be in the eyes of others impacted by this decision? An overriding question ought to be: Why am I considering the involvement of others in this decision? If you can't think of a good reason for the inclusion of others, it might be that you don't need to engage them in the decision. (And of course if you haven't assessed the situation objectively then you are probably just deluding yourself!)

AT THE SCREEN FACE ...

Using social media to create organizational conversations

Peter Williams is the "chief edge officer" at Deloitte Australia, and "a great believer in the transformational power of social media at the organisational and individual level," wrote Padmer Iyer in *The Australian*:

"In organisations often the left hand didn't know what the right hand was doing and people worked in different groups and tended only to interact with people they came into contact with on a day-to-day basis,' Williams says.

'When you bring social software into the workplace and people start participating in it, you are going to ask, "Does anybody know anything about this topic?" or "Does anybody know this person?" or "I have got a problem ... can you give me input?"

'We suddenly see an organisation become an ecosystem or a network as opposed to an organisational chart. It has a profound impact on people's sense of being part of something bigger, people's ability to follow their passion.'"[1]

Leaders get criticized for involving others too much and too little in the decision-making process; it is often hard to strike the right balance. If your personal preference favors allowing others the freedom and autonomy to make their own decisions, people may think – or worse, say – you are "not across the details" or "not in the loop" or "out of touch." This could of course be valid criticism. Valid or invalid, it is a negative perception others may hold, based on your preferred leadership style.

Then again, if you are somewhat reluctant to involve others in decision-making – particularly your team – you may be open to criticism of being too autocratic. Your team will consider you to be a "micromanager" or too interfering. A unilateral decision-making style can create an impression, rightly or wrongly, that you are too hands-on and mistrusting of your team and/or disrespectful of their ability to take appropriate action without you.

Like all leadership styles and approaches, it pays to be flexible and adaptable. Decision-making is no different. To be an effective decision-maker, being prepared to use all three approaches, depending on the circumstances and the people you are working with, is a good starting point. Being flexible means a preparedness and willingness to use all three decision-making approaches. It means having the ability to assess the situation and the people involved. Adaptability means a preparedness, willingness, and ability to shift from one approach to another when the situation calls for it. Each of these approaches involves a different style of communication.

Figure 8.1 illustrates the three main approaches to decision-making we mentioned earlier: *Consultative*, *Collaborative*, and *Enabling*.

At one end of the continuum (left-hand side) the focus is squarely on the decision-making *task*; that is, deciding primarily on the best course of action to get a task accomplished. At the other end of the continuum (right-hand side) is *relationships* involved in the decision; that is, the focus is first and foremost on maintaining good working relationships with those affected by the decision. In

FIGURE 8.1 / **Decision-making approaches**

the middle of these two extremes is an equal consideration of the task and relationships.

Let's examine each approach more closely.

/ Consultative decision-making

Consultative decision-making emphasizes task over the relationships. With the consultative dimension, deciding on the correct course of action takes precedence over relationship considerations. Usually this form of decision-making relies on seeking the expert advice of someone else to make an informed decision.

For instance, consider the situation where a CEO has to make a decision on whether to dismiss an employee for misconduct. Before taking action, the CEO consults with the HR manager who is an expert in industrial relations and law. The HR manager then advises the CEO of the range of options and the CEO then makes a decision based on that advice. The focus of consultative decision-making is about making the right decision based on input from others.

Leaders in these task-specific quandaries seek out advice from others with certain expertise or knowledge, a proven track record, or past experience in similar cases. When consulting with others, the leader's interaction is based on eliciting important and relevant information to guide and inform their decision. The aim of these consultative conversations is to draw out the right information to make an informed decision.

The dialogue in the consultative conversation will necessarily follow a question–answer structure. The person seeking advice asks specific questions related to the task-at-hand and the expert responds. By asking a series of open-ended questions, the leader is hoping to draw out the relevant information required to take the right course-of-action. The purpose of consultative dialogue is to be guided, informed, educated, or enlightened about a matter the leader has less knowledge of or insight about than the person or persons they are consulting. So the quality of the dialogue is based on the questions and responses. Of course, this is based on the assumption that the "expert" has the answers and the capacity and willingness to communicate this information, as well as the leader knowing what questions to ask.

Consider this example of when a consultative decision-making approach is apt.

Ted is general manager of a large civil engineering consultancy firm. He has been asked by one of his major clients to change the plans for the construction of a shopping center. Ted understands that this alteration in the specifications is significant and will consequently take more time and cost more than the deadlines and fees stated in the current contract. The client acknowledges this in his conversation with Ted; he is willing to accept a fee increase and time delay. But are these changes feasible from a construction perspective?

Ted needs to consult with the expert, in this case, his project director. Bill is the project director. During the conversation between Ted and Bill, Bill assures Ted that the work can be carried out and provides a clear estimate of the additional timeframe and adjusted cost for the project's completion. Based on this expertise, Ted decides that he can accept the client's new change-of-plan.

Ted subsequently informs his client of this information and a contract variation is drawn up to accommodate these alterations in the construction of the shopping center.

In this case, it wasn't Bill's decision to make as the project manager; it was Ted's decision as general manager. Ted nevertheless had to consult with Bill to determine feasibility of the client's request. He also needed to provide the client with an accurate indication of the fee increase and time delay. The conversation was focused on the task rather than preserving or building a better working relationship between the general manager and his project manager.

Collaborative decision-making

Collaborative decision-making involves balancing the task-at-hand with the relationships of the people with a clear vested interest in the decision. It involves making a collective decision with one or more persons. A collaborative decision is a shared decision. The collaborative conversation centers on problem-solving and coming up with a resolution that two or more people in the conversation are willing to commit to.

Decisions that are made collaboratively take into consideration getting a particular task accomplished and maintaining harmonious working relationships between key stakeholders. The leader's overriding aim is to come up with a quality decision that one or more participants own.

Collaborative conversations are less structured than a consultative conversation and the dialogue more free flowing. For genuine collaboration to take place, everyone – whether two or twenty people – ought to be given the opportunity to contribute to the conversation. People may not take the invitation to have a say, particularly in conversations involving groups; while others may want to contribute more than others. But all participants in the collaborative conversation are invited to contribute – and should be expected to.

Because of their more broad-ranging nature, collaborative conversations must have a clear purpose. Clarifying the purpose of the conversation is the responsibility of the leader. For instance, a leader might say at the outset of a team meeting: "The objective of this meeting is to come up with a decision to this problem we are facing. I want us to make a decision that we are all prepared to commit to." When these kinds of conversations inevitably meander off topic, the leader's other important role, apart from articulating the purpose, is to guide the participants back to the purpose. As we mentioned earlier, collaborative decision-making is a delicate balancing act. On the one hand, the leader wants a quality outcome; the task emphasis. On the other hand, the leader needs to be mindful of ensuring that everyone is given a fair opportunity to contribute to the conversation; which is the relationships dimension. Briefly, the leader's role in collaborative conversations is to balance taking action and being mindful of human interactions.

There are a variety of occasions when collaborative decision-making is useful. In circumstances where a team or individual will be directly affected by a decision and have a vested interest in its outcome, a collaborative discussion is fitting. Collaboration demonstrates respect and consideration for the views of others.

By collaborating with several people, the leader is opening up the possibility of surfacing differing perspectives and strongly held opinions. If a collaborative conversation can't resolve the issue, the leader may need to adapt to a consultative approach and make the decision, having heard the views of all stakeholders. Having attempted unsuccessfully to make a collective decision, the team will probably understand the need for the leader to change their approach. Whilst some may not agree with the leader's ultimate decision, they should at least understand the necessity to change approaches. Even so, in the first instance sensitive decisions that dramatically impact on others are often best resolved collaboratively.

For example, Sarah has a team of five supervisors who work across three shifts in a production company. She wants to set the roster for the next quarter and realizes that her supervisors will have a variety of preferences for the shifts they wish to supervise. Sarah calls a meeting and reviews the roster with her five supervisors. She knows that the roster probably won't please all five supervisors. But she also wants to be fair to her team members. A collaborative conversation encourages her team to work together to fill the roster. Sarah is mindful of completing the roster (task) and – at the same time – respecting the rights of her supervisors (relationships).

Enabling decision-making

At the other end of the spectrum to the consultative approach, *enabling decision-making* (right-hand side of Figure 8.1) is very much focused on maintaining and building working relationships. There is a fundamental difference between the consultative and collaborative approaches already discussed and enabling conversations. The consultative and collaborative conversations are usually initiated by the leader, whereas the enabling conversation is often started by others, such as team members. In other words, the enabling conversation usually involves reacting and responding to others. The consultative and collaborative approaches on the other hand are usually more proactive initiatives; these are dialogues initiated by the leader.

Enabling decision-making will typically start with someone seeking advice from their manager on a decision they need to make. From the perspective of the initiator, their approach to their manager is consultative. But instead of giving advice to a team member, the manager turns the interaction from a consultative to enabling conversation. The leader permits the team member to make the decision, reassures the team member about their capacity to make the decision (encouraging conversation, *see* Chapter 6), or provides some guidance to help them to make the decision. But they avoid making the decision for the person.

For instance, a team member is having interpersonal difficulties with one of their team colleagues. They come to their manager wanting them to resolve the conflict. But instead of doing so, the manager uses a series of thought-provoking questions to encourage the team member to arrive at their own decision on how best to fix the problem. Questions such as: "Besides approaching me, what else could you do to sort this conflict out with Mary?", shifting the conversation from consultative to enabling. This question helps the team member to consider other options, enabling them to take greater responsibility.

After an enabling conversation with their manager, a team member may feel a sense of empowerment to respond effectively to a problem, dilemma, or decision. This decision-making approach is about helping the team member to arrive at a course-of-action. By having an enabling conversation, the leader encourages the team member to think of their own solution and act upon it. Through an enabling conversation, the manager's focus is on dialogue that promotes trust and confidence in – and respect for – the team member. The emphasis is on the relationship.

Enabling conversations encourage others to decide for themselves. The onus of responsibility is on the other party to decide on a way forward rather than on the leader deciding or recommending. In this conversation, the leader's role is one of support and facilitation that assists the person or team to arrive at a decision they are comfortable with.

With a relationships focus, the leader is mindful that directly imposing a solution may adversely affect their working relationship with others. This shouldn't be seen as a convenient excuse to avoid tough decisions. The goal in enabling decision-making is two-fold. First, it encourages others to take charge of their circumstances. And second, by demonstrating faith in the capacity of other people to resolve an issue, the leader is strengthening their interpersonal relationships with their team members. In a nutshell, the enabling conversation is about encouraging others to take responsibility and act.

Enabling conversations support individuals and teams to act, but may also require managers to clarify the parameters of decision-making. Where are the boundaries for autonomous decision-making? What are the non-negotiable factors that need to be considered when taking action? Within these practical concerns and necessary constraints, enabling others to make their own decisions is a vote of confidence from the leader in the ability of others to deal with an issue.

For example, Jim is the sales director of a large chain of retail stores. He has a team of salespeople scattered across the country servicing their local business communities. Jim sees his role as one of setting realistic targets for his sales staff. He is perfectly happy for them all to manage their own territories in a way they see fit. Jim knows that his sales team are all experienced, with proven track records. He is aware that his salespeople know their territories well; they have sound local knowledge. So the majority of Jim's conversations with team members are around the individual budgets he has set for each of them, and the progress they are making in meeting these targets. His conversations are mostly about enabling others to meet these targets, drawing on their own local knowledge and sales experience.

Let's now turn to conversations about reviewing targets, decisions, and actions.

Reviewing targets, decisions, and actions

If targets are not reviewed, then it is pretty much pointless deciding on them in the first place. Essentially, reviewing targets and actions can be done in four ways. Table 8.1 illustrates these four options.

In Table 8.1, *formative* refers to an ongoing target review process. *Summative*, on the other hand, is reviewing targets at the end of the project. On the right-hand side, *informal* refers to the *ad hoc* approach to reviewing targets. *Formal* is a more structured and systematic review of targets. As you can see in the table, this provides a leader with four options when reviewing targets or action: *regular dialogue*; *following procedures*; *end of project debrief*; or *end of project presentation*.

We will elaborate on each of these options in reviewing action.

Regular dialogue

Regular dialogue means reviewing targets frequently in a casual way. This form of appraisal could apply in a situation where a manager is working with a small group of highly-skilled operators. They may choose to check in casually at the end of the day or week over several weeks with their team. This could be done in an unstructured

TABLE 8.1   Target reviewing options[2]

Formative	Summative	
Regular dialogue	End of project debrief	*Informal*
Following procedures	End of project presentation	*Formal*

conversation over coffee, for example. Predetermined targets can be reinforced by the leader at these informal interactions, and agreements reached. Through these regular casual conversations, the manager has the opportunity to practice an informal kind of influence.[3]

Following procedures

Following procedures also means reviewing targets on a regular basis, but doing so in a structured and systematic way. This may take the form of a series of frequent, formal review meetings. Following procedures is a useful review process when there is a fair degree of complexity in a project, involving a wide variety of stakeholders. In these circumstances, a more structured dialogue process is more appropriate.

End of project debrief

The end of project debrief refers to appraising targets at the completion of a project, but doing so in a less structured way. This target review approach is suitable for relatively simple matters where the participants have demonstrated a high degree of competence. The manager in these cases can check in with his or her team to ensure that targets have been met.

End of project presentation

Lastly, the end of project presentation, as its name implies, is also carried out once a project has been finished, done in formal written or verbal reporting format. This approach to reviewing would occur when the manager wants to ensure that several predetermined standards and milestones have been met. The project team members are subsequently expected to respond in writing or verbally to a set of criteria. These criteria have been agreed upon before the project's commencement. These conversations are more formal and more closely resemble typical formal organizational interaction.

Turning our attention to reviewing action, we can't think of a better technique for this than the After Action Review.

After Action Review

A powerful technique for reviewing action is called an After Action Review. According to management guru, Peter Senge, in *The Dance of Change*:

> The Army's After Action Review (AAR) is arguably one of the most successful organizational learning methods yet devised. Yet, most every corporate effort to graft this truly innovative practice into their culture has failed because, again and again, people reduce the living practice of AAR's to a sterile technique.[4]

High praise indeed. And an important cautionary note.

So what exactly is an AAR?

The AAR is a debriefing methodology that assists in learning the lessons of the past to make improvements in processes and procedures for the future. As a technique, it can be applied at any of the four reviewing stages in Table 8.1 above. Specifically, it can be done formatively during a project, or summatively at the conclusion of the project. The AAR can be applied informally or formally as well. So its application is very adaptable.

The spirit of an AAR is one of openness and learning; it is not about problem-fixing or allocating blame. Lessons learned are not only tacitly shared on the spot by the individuals involved in a project or task, but can be explicitly documented and communicated for a wider audience. AARs were originally developed and are still extensively used by the US Army and other military organizations around the world, including the Singapore Armed Forces.

What makes AARs so powerful is that they can be applied across a wide spectrum of activities, from two individuals conducting a five-minute AAR at the end of a short meeting to a day-long AAR held off-site by a project team at the end of a large-scale project. This reflects Senge's observation about the value of AARs when they become part of the culture, rather than simply a technique. Activities suitable for AARs simply need to have a fixed beginning and end, an identifiable purpose and some basis on which performance can be assessed.

There are many versions of the AAR. But the one that we think is most applicable for managers is based on the following three simple but important questions:

1. What went well (or is going well) in the project?
2. What did not (or is not) going well in the project?
3. What lessons can we apply in the future from our experiences?

These three questions focus the minds of project participants on reviewing key aspects of project implementation. As we mentioned earlier, these questions can be addressed casually or formally as part of a set meeting. Apart from gleaning the gems of wisdom gained from the experiences of a project, the AAR also generates a sense of commitment from those who participate. This is because it is done collaboratively. The AAR is a practical tool for collaborative dialogue.

Here are some examples of when an AAR can be used:

- When a manager is introducing a new set of procedures or ways of working, and after the new ways are in place.
- After a busy period of time when capacity was stretched, and during times of stretch to monitor how things are going.
- During and following the introduction of a new system or procedure.
- After a major training activity.
- After a shift handover.

This list is by no means conclusive. Nonetheless, it does provide some practical situations in which the AAR can be employed.

An AAR is excellent for making tacit knowledge explicit during the life of a project or activity. It provides a vehicle for the leader to capture ideas from team members and endorse suggestions for adapting approaches. Learning can also be summarized before a team disbands, or before people forget what happened and move on to something else. Despite the name ("after action"), it doesn't have to be performed at the end of a project or activity; rather, it can be performed after each identifiable milestone within a cycle of a project or major activity. Doing an AAR at discernible phases means it becomes a live learning process whereby lessons learned can be immediately applied. This is where AARs can add great value as a tool for providing feedback.

AARs can also be used for conscious and directed personal reflection. For example, take a few minutes to reflect on something you did yesterday, such as meeting with an important stakeholder, dealing with a complaint, or making an important telephone call. Ask yourself the three AAR questions above. What does the AAR tell you about what you could do differently tomorrow? This stimulates constructive internal dialogue.

A T   T H E   C O A L   F A C E   ...

The Atlantic incident: Management response and the after action review

In one of the authors' previous books, *The New Influencing Toolkit: Capabilities for Communicating with Influence*, the following case study is featured. It illustrates the effectiveness of the AAR as a tool of dialogue.

An After Action Review (AAR) was conducted on 15 March at the State Forestry Offices in Dry Branch, Georgia. The Fish and Wildlife Service, Forest Service, Georgia State Forestry, State Air Protection Branch, EPA, and media were all represented, in addition to members of the public and the prescribed burning community.

The atmosphere just prior to the AAR appeared to be rather contentious. However, as the AAR commenced, the Forest Service began not by denying any blame for the incident, but by apologizing for any inconvenience their burn had caused the public. That statement helped to make the participants from the air regulatory community much more willing to work together to describe and solve the problem in a cooperative manner.

While both prescribed burns were performed consistent with directions, it was clear that the existing tools for predicting, measuring, modeling, and managing prescribed burning at the regional level were insufficient. This is evidenced in the process of issuing burn permits at the time. While both the Piedmont and Oconee received permits from the same office, it is unclear if the office was aware of the concurrent burns. The Georgia Forestry Commission issues burn permits from 130 offices throughout the state in the absence of coordination between the separate offices.

The AAR resulted in the following recommendations:

Establish certified smoke management program for Georgia.
Have the Georgia Forestry Commission manage permitting more regionally than locally.

Track permits real time for air quality management.

Communicate large acreage permits to the media.

Support accelerated USDA-Forest Service research for new smoke modeling.

Improve meteorology and modeling for regional air quality management of prescribed burning.

Assemble more data on the health impacts of such an intrusion on the metro area.

Gather data on local Atlanta emissions from fire impacts on such an intrusion.

Increase public education regarding prescribed burning especially for audiences in non-attainment areas.[5]

This brings us to the conclusion of Chapter 8 and Part II. We have covered some of the important considerations for having conversations about decision-making and reviewing targets and action. Action-orientated conversations can be classified as consultative, collaborative, or enabling. Selecting the best approach depends on two important variables: the situation you are facing and the type of action or decision needed, and the other person or people involved in the decision. Although, as we have pointed out, your bias towards one of these three approaches is likely to influence your choice, often subconsciously. We also covered the four dimensions of reviewing targets and the use of an AAR.

We are now ready to move to Part III. In this final part of our book, we look at the skills of conversations. This is done by illustrating a model of communication we refer to as the *Face of Communication*. The model is used to highlight the importance and value of perception and nonverbal communication, listening, asking questions, and safe, open feedback channels. In this section of the book, we'll explore each of these everyday communication principles and behaviors, showing their simple but powerful significance in building practical management conversation skills.

The **Top 10** Key Points …

 Managerial decision-making involving others can be classified in one of three ways: decisions that require consultation and input from others; decisions that are made collaboratively with others; and decisions made by others with some input from the manager.

Consultative decision-making relies on seeking expert advice of someone else to make a quality decision.

Collaborative decision-making involves making a decision collectively with one or more persons.

Enabling decision-making is encouraging others to make their own decisions.

The first of four ways of reviewing action is regular dialogue, meaning reviewing targets frequently in a casual way.

The second way is following procedures, meaning reviewing targets on a regular basis, but doing so in a structured and systematic way.

The third way is an end of project debrief, which refers to appraising targets at the completion of a project, but doing so in a less structured way.

The fourth and final way of reviewing action is an end of project presentation, which, as its name implies, is carried out once a project has been finished, and done in a formal written or verbal reporting format.

An after action review is a debriefing methodology that assists in learning the lessons of the past to make improvements in processes and procedures for the future.

The AAR is a practical tool for generating collaborative dialogue.

part III

The Skills of Conversations

chapter 9

The "Face" of Communication

One way to think about our communication skills is to look in the mirror and see what our face has to tell us. It's a practical cue we can use every day to focus on some powerful communication behaviors.

In this short chapter, we want to introduce you to a model: the *Face of Communication*. Features of the model will be used to consider some of the key skills in managing conversations in Chapters 10 to 14 in Part III.

When people converse – in Western cultures at least – they naturally look at each other's face. And that instinctive act can serve as a simple but effective reminder about some key, but often overlooked, elements of effective interpersonal communication – whether at work or home. One way to think about our communication skills is to look in the mirror and see what our face has to tell us. The features of our face offer some practical cues we can use every day to focus on some powerful communication behaviors.

Figure 9.1 illustrates the Face of Communication.

Using the features of our ears, eyes, nose, and mouth as everyday visual reminders to ourselves, we can sketch four key communication

FIGURE 9.1 Face of communication

principles and skills, each of which will be a subject of the following chapters in Part III.

Listening to understand

It has been noted many times that we have *two ears* and one mouth. Yet while listening is one of the most powerful aspects of communication and relationship building, it's also probably the most neglected. Chapter 10 refers to the ears in the Face of Communication model. Conversations can't exist without listening, and more productive conversations start with listening to the other person more attentively. Listening means more than simply hearing, it's about our attention, our focus, and our connection with what the other person is trying to say.

Watching our own and others' behaviors

The *eyes* highlight the importance of attention-giving and the nonverbal aspects of communication. Chapter 11 considers three perceptual positions we can be in during dialogue; the third position being the most constructive in conversation. Chapter 12 reminds us that we don't only listen with our ears, we can also listen with our eyes as we observe important nonverbal messages that people are sending. The eyes also remind us that we are being observed when we communicate, highlighting that what we communicate consists of much more than just what we say.

Asking questions

The *nose*, represented by the upturned question mark (used in Spanish at the start of sentences that ask a question), illustrates that learning conversations require questioning skills. Conversation is far more than just turn-taking information exchange. Chapter 13 covers the vital ingredients of reflection, investigation, and integration in conversations.

Safe, open feedback channels

And finally, the smiling *mouth* shape illustrates the need for information to flow in both directions; that safe, open feedback channels are at the heart of authentic conversations. Chapter 14 provides some tips on creating the safety required for communication to flow smoothly in both directions.

In Part III, we'll explore the use of each of these everyday communication principles and behaviors, showing their simple but powerful roles in enabling richer conversations and relationships.

chapter 10

Active Listening Can Make Other People Better Communicators Too

Listening is sometimes called "the neglected communication skill" – perhaps because it looks easy, passive, and instinctive. Experience tells us, however, that it's anything but. It takes effort, energy, and skill to be a good listener. But the rewards are well worth the effort. And not only because it makes us better communicators – effective listening can help other people communicate better too.

The University of Massachusetts conducted an experiment in which they trained six students in "attending skills" – such as an interested posture and eye contact. Then they recorded a lecture the students attended with a visiting professor. The students were told to adopt typical non-attending student behaviors at the beginning of the lecture. The professor lectured from his notes, spoke in a monotone and paid little attention to the students. According to Ivey and Hinkle, "At a prearranged signal, however, the students began deliberately to physically attend. Within half a minute, the lecturer gestured for the first time, his verbal rate increased, and a lively classroom session was born. Simple attending had changed the whole picture. At another signal, the students stopped attending, and the speaker, after awkwardly *seeking continued response, resumed the un-engaging lecture with which he began the class."[1]*

This simple experiment highlights several important principles of effective communication. One is that other people notice how we listen and adapt their communication to our listening. Directly related to that is the fact that our listening – aural, visual, and physical – influences the quality of others' communication. And it reinforces the point that listening is, really, a lot more than simply hearing.

So, if you want to experience better, richer, more interesting and informative, productive conversations – listen more attentively! Listening is sometimes called "the neglected communication skill" – perhaps because it looks easy, passive, and instinctive. Experience tells us, however, that it's anything but. It takes effort, energy, and skill to be a good listener. But the rewards are well worth the effort. And not only because it makes us better communicators – listening effectively can help other people communicate better too.

You will have noticed that listening is a theme woven throughout this book. That's not surprising in a book about the role and power of conversation as a tool of communication. It reminds us of how ubiquitous listening is – or should be – in our communication. Unfortunately, the expectations are often much higher than the actual experience. The important thing is to understand why listening is so important – and to appreciate why it's so easy for us to take it for granted rather than intentionally investing our energy in listening attentively.

"Active listening" engages our senses in a concerted effort to tune into the other person so that we can receive their message. Listening actively is not simply a physical activity – it is an act of will. Listening effectively requires self-directed motivation to listen, and self-management while we listen.

Listening is hard work

Okay, so I want to listen, but still it's hard. I really try to pay attention but I seem to be distracted by passers-by, stray thoughts, the speaker's mannerisms … and my thoughts about what I'm going to say next. And anyway, what am I supposed to do while the other person is talking? What is listening anyway? And what makes some listening "active"?

First, consider this challenging reality. The average rate of speech is somewhere between about 120 and 170 words per minute. You can probably think of friends and colleagues at either end of the range. Now the challenge: the human brain has a far greater capacity to process information than the typical rate of speech presents it with. For example, many people can easily read at 200–300 words per minute and with training can comprehend double that many. There's no definitive number, but it's estimated the human brain at least has the capacity to process the equivalent of twice the normal rate of speech and probably a lot more. You can instantly see the problem: there's a gap between the ponderous rate at which people speak and the lightning speed of our mental processing as listeners.

"Managing the gap" is what active listening is about. Because if you don't manage it, all those passers-by, stray thoughts, and speaker's mannerisms (not to mention your mental to-do list about the movie you want to catch, or whether you'll make the early train) will fill in that gap and you will be widening the gulf between yourself and your speaker. Not to mention understanding what it is they mean.

Listening is hard for everyone. Not just Type A personalities. Not just very busy people. Not just leaders with many responsibilities. Everyone has to manage the gap. But of course for those attempting to create and sustain rich, productive leadership conversations, the stakes are higher. Once people decide you're not paying attention they'll be polite, they'll share what they need to, and fulfill their responsibilities – but they won't expend the effort to share richer information. It's not hard to pick up the cue that someone is too busy, thinks they're too important or are just too distracted for what we think they need to know. And so the "listener" distractedly carries on without the benefit of the additional information they could have been given if they'd been willing to *really* listen.

It's no surprise that as our responsibilities increase, our work increasingly involves communication. Or that our effectiveness depends upon our ability to communicate. What does surprise some people is that the actual communication behaviors or skills we need to use as our responsibilities increase require greater amounts of, and attention to, listening. That is, as our roles become more accountable and carry more authority so too does the need for effective listening increase.

"Listening is the front end of decision making," writes Bernard T. Ferrari, author of *Power Listening: Mastering the most critical business skill of all*:

> Good listening – the active and disciplined activity of probing and challenging the information garnered from others to improve its quality and quantity – is the key to building a base of knowledge that generates fresh insights and ideas.[2]

It's hard to disagree with Ferrari. But that doesn't necessarily make it any easier to do. Listening is hard work.

What makes listening a challenge for many of us is that we struggle to allow others to advance, explore, and discover their own thinking, and create new possibilities. Our own mental frames and assumptions are potent and our instinct is to assume these mindsets are "right." And while we would all claim to be committed to values such as "respect," "diversity," and "learning," it's not until we are prepared to stop and listen that we actually demonstrate our commitment to those principles.

But stopping and listening are almost counterintuitive to the way much interaction takes place in our busy, distracted workplaces. This leads to what Daniel Goleman calls the "common cold of the workplace": tuning out of what the other person is saying before we fully understand – and telling them what we think too soon. "Real listening means hearing the person out and then responding, in a mutual dialogue," says Goleman.[3]

We've all suffered with that "common cold." And we've all seen others suffering with it – no matter the season of the year. Listening is one of the hardest things we have to do when we communicate. And before you dismiss this as a statement of the obvious, think about how hard it is to listen when:

- You already "know" what they mean.
- You have something constructive and valuable to contribute.
- You need the other person to know how much you know about an event, topic, or situation.
- You think the other person has had a fair go and has been talking long enough.
- You urgently have something else to do or somewhere else you need to be.

Another way to test the depth of your listening capacity is to identify a time recently when you were genuinely completely focused on another person's message. That means: no distracting thoughts, no interrupting, and no split attention. For most of us, those experiences of a total state of consciousness – what Mihaly Csikszentmihalyi called "Flow" – in the message of someone else, are rare. And even if you consider yourself a pretty good listener (surveys show most of us do think this about ourselves), it's probably difficult to think of more than a handful of recent occasions when someone else listened to you in the ways described above.

Despite the popular rhetoric, poor listening is not a recent phenomenon. Back in the 1950s, Dr Ralph G. Nichols, from the University of Minnesota, tested the ability of people to listen for understanding. The results have found their way into much subsequent commentary on communication and learning:

> It can be stated with practically no qualification that people in general do not know how to listen. They have ears that hear very well, but seldom have they acquired the necessary ... skills which would allow those ears to be used effectively for what is called listening ... For several years, we have been testing the ability of people to understand and remember what they hear ... These extensive tests led to this general conclusion: immediately after the average person has listened to someone talk, he [sic] remembers only about half of what he has heard – no matter how carefully he thought he was listening.[4]

So yes, listening is more difficult than we think. Even when we are genuinely interested in what's being said, listening is easier said than done. This is because good listening means blocking out everything else. It requires the focus of our brains, our bodies, and our hearts. It requires a concentration of energy.

And energy is a precious resource, so we can easily tell ourselves it will be more productive if we ration our attention and "multitask" while we *listen*. "Keep talking," we say as we put the finishing touches to an email or peek at a text message, "I'm listening." And we are being genuine; we believe it. But the other person doesn't believe it. They know – as we do when someone does the same thing to us – that we can't listen and do another cognitive task at the same time. It's either one task or the other. We talk about the necessity to "walk and chew gum at the same time," but we can't actually multitask cognitive processes. We can switch between mental processes. But this means we don't do either task as well as we would if we did one with total attentiveness. So ironically, multitasking is inefficient and slower than doing one cerebral job at a time. Yet we have convinced ourselves that doing two challenging tasks at a time is more productive.

AT THE COAL FACE ...

Who is really important?

During a workshop one of us conducted with a group of food manufacturing managers, we offered the following reflective exercise.

Write down a list of the most significant people in your life right now. They can be from work, family, friends, or community. First names are all you need. Try to write down at least 15–20 names.

Now assess how well you typically listen to each of these people, maybe considering how they might describe how well you listen to them.

What surprised the managers in the workshop was how poorly they typically listened to the people who were most significant in their lives – especially their family. It was easier to show respectful attention and listen carefully to people they had just met, new clients, or someone apparently important or famous but who had little real significance to them. In discussing their reflections they concluded that it becomes easy to make assumptions about those we think we know best, to take the relationship for granted, to assume we know what they are thinking or what they mean or what they are likely to say.

How about you?

L.I.S.T.E.N.E.R.

Now the good news: None of us needs to remain captive to substandard listening behaviors. There are practical things we can do (or not do) in every conversation to improve our own listening capability. Apart from helping ourselves improve our communication, we can also help others to improve their communication with us. These new habits are largely about being more self-aware and being prepared to self-manage. Like most things, it does require some focus and effort. Sadly, unlike some other improvements and achievements we can make, it is unlikely anyone will ever give us an award for being an awesome listener! But they will be aware of it and the effectiveness of our influence with them and our relationship with them will improve. And that is its own valuable reward. It is difficult to listen consistently well, and impossible to do it perfectly. But we all are capable of improving. Even a couple of small intentional improvements can have a multiplier effect on the quality of our conversations and relationships.

Following is a short contribution to your continuing development of effective listening skills as a key part of effective leadership. It's in the form of an acronym: LISTENER.

No doubt you do some of these things well already, so go ahead and give yourself a pat on the back for those when you notice yourself applying them in your upcoming conversations. There are also probably one or two that you know you struggle with. You know these are capabilities that could be enhanced and that you could be more intentional about them. Mark those for attention and try to intentionally practice them in the conversations you have immediately after identifying them.

Look for

Listening isn't really a passive activity. *Look for* reminds us that good listening takes active involvement. One practical way to do that is to look for answers in your conversations. Focus on what's being said and look for connections and links to the issues and questions at hand. Asking questions of the speaker indicates that you're engaged with what they are saying and listened carefully in the conversation. Questions not only clarify things for you, they can clarify the other person's thinking too. In the context of respectful listening, looking for answers to questions positively challenges your own and the other person's thinking. Learning requires some reflection, and reflection means seeking out answers and asking thought-provoking questions. Looking for answers shifts your listening mindset from passive receptor to active participant in the conversation and helps to manage the listening–speaking gap.

Information removal

Busyness is a perennial challenge for everyone now; we are all bombarded with too much information from numerous directions. Information overload affects and afflicts us all every day. Giving your attention to someone or something necessarily requires that we choose to focus on what they are trying to inform us about, rather than allowing other information to block or interfere with their message. Where you focus your attention is ultimately a choice you make or don't make; that is, you inevitably focus on something and not something else. The question is how conscious and in control of your attention you choose to be. *Information removal* is the idea of postponing the conversation until you have removed the distractions you currently have in front of you. Oftentimes, the smartest course of action you can take is to deal with the immediate situation you are facing first before being sucked into another conversation. Let the person who wants to discuss a matter with you know that you need to sort out and remove a problem straightaway. Indicate that you will discuss their matter with them at a convenient time. Far from being disrespectful or dismissive, this actually lets them know that you place a value on your communication with them and want to be able to focus appropriately. You might simply trying saying, "Now's not a good time, can we reschedule so we can give this our full attention?" And once you have eliminated the overload of information – whether it is an email, conference call, another conversation you are facing, or something else – make time to seek out that person to discuss their matter. This communicates respect for the person and their agenda, as well as for your own responsibilities.

A T   T H E   S C R E E N   F A C E   ...

One screen at a time

All of us have experienced the competing commitments of sitting at our desks and conversing with a person or group of people on conference call. Even when you can see faces by video, it's challenging to keep track of the conversation when people are not in physical proximity around the table. And there's a natural temptation that arises when you know others can't see everything you're doing or hear what you're saying when you are on "mute":

checking out other work or having a sidebar conversation. While it makes perfect sense to us as we "multitask," it rarely makes sense to us if we think others are doing it while we're talking!

Remote conferencing technologies open up great opportunities for real-time conversations across distances and time zones, but those opportunities are sabotaged if we don't apply the same listening and attention principles as we should to face-to-face conversations.

One way to self-manage this is to follow a practice used by coaches who use the telephone or video calls to coach. This involves ensuring that what the coach can see on their desk is only related to the coaching session, and communicating a visual description of their environment to the person they're coaching. This reassures the coachee that the coach is totally focused on them, as well as sending the message that they should reciprocate. That includes ensuring secondary screens like phones or tablets are switched off. One screen at a time supports focused, attentive, professional listening.

Silence

We can't talk and listen at the same time. And that includes talking to yourself! So *silence* your voice and *silence* the voice in your head (you know, the one that has all the answers before the other person has finished) so you can create clear mental space for genuine listening. For many of us, silence is disconcerting, so we do things like "helpfully" finishing others' sentences, or rushing to inject our own comment rather than pausing to acknowledge what the other person has just said or see if they want to continue.

Many of our counterparts in conversation are, of course, very comfortable with silence and actually use it as a means of assessing whether or not we are really listening to them and are engaged in the conversation. Silence is actually a powerful tool in communication – as negotiators, counselors, and coaches all know. Our ability to appropriately use silence in conversations can be significantly improved with intent and practice. Silence demonstrates another source of respect for the speaker.

Target

Setting yourself a *target* or purpose when you are listening to someone else helps considerably to motivate your listening efforts because it gives you a reason and focus for listening. Your target might be, for example, to show your support, to encourage someone to deal with a problem, or to understand a point-of-view you don't agree with. Or maybe your target is to improve your listening skills! Just as we ought to read with a purpose, we should listen with an aim or target in mind.

Encourage

During a conversation, *encourage* the other person with verbal acknowledgments and nonverbal gestures. Nonverbal gestures include facing the person you are conversing with, leaning forward slightly, and maintaining appropriate eye contact. Nodding to let them know you are listening is another nonverbal way of encouraging the person to continue, as is the use of appropriate facial gestures (concern, surprise, and understanding). All of these signals encourage the person you are conversing with to elaborate and engage at a deeper level. Verbal comments such as "I see," "that's interesting," "tell me about ...," "go on," create a positive and affirming climate. These encouraging words and gestures allow you to open up, deepen, and broaden the conversation.

Narrate

Narrate refers to relating to the speaker by sharing the narrative or story they are sharing. There are several ways to do this. One of the best ways is to occasionally use the speaker's own words. For instance, if they use phrases such as "critically important" or a "challenging situation," inject these into your dialogue. "I can see why you think this is critically important" or "You are right, this is a challenging situation." Using the speaker's words not only communicates that you have heard them, it also confirms that you are on the same wavelength as them because you are using expressions they are familiar with. Narrating also provides a bridge to challenging, endorsing, or further exploring their words and ideas. As the listener, narrating or recounting their expressions helps you reinforce for yourself what the other person is saying, meaning you are managing your attention and mindset more effectively.

Emotions

Emotions influence not only the way we express ourselves, but also the way we listen. When a topic is something we feel strongly about, our emotional responses can filter what we hear and pay attention to. In emotionally-charged interaction, it pays to be aware of and manage your own emotional reactions as best you can. Self-awareness and self-management are keys to emotional intelligence, because we cannot think clearly (and therefore cannot communicate effectively) if our brains have been emotionally hijacked. Awareness and management of our own emotions also gives us a sense of emotional control to be able to acknowledge how we feel so we don't adversely react to others' emotions. Emotional intelligence in conversations also enables us to acknowledge and appropriately respond to others' emotional language and behavior, again providing valuable control in otherwise highly-charged exchanges.

Respect

Respect is the last of our eight pointers in our LISTENER acronym. It reminds us that effective conversations require respect – for the other person, for the topic being discussed, and for ourselves. It also reminds us that even good techniques (like verbal and nonverbal encouraging, or narrating, or looking for answers) will have limited effect if we don't listen with respect. That's because conversation is an interpersonal exchange between human beings. Each of the previous seven capabilities is a form of respect for the person you are conversing with, as well as for yourself. Managing external distractions is an important but often overlooked part of quality listening. It is actually about showing *respect*. Shutting a door, turning off a phone, or finding a quieter place to listen are all simple but powerful actions that improve the communication exchange. They enhance the conversation not only because of the elimination or minimization of interruption, but also because they convey a message of respect for the other party. Likewise, giving your focused attention, sharing the narrative, and respecting emotions shows respect in the sense that you are making it clear that the other person is important and that you value them and what they have to say.

Listening is a choice, just as all of the pointers we've looked at are choices. Even focusing more intentional effort on just one of these listening skills – *Look for, Information removal, Silence, Target, Encourage, Narrate, Emotions, Respect* (LISTENER) – can have a profound impact on the quality of your conversations. But a word of warning. Be prepared for some interesting reactions from people who may be unaccustomed to you being so attentive, managing the environment more consciously, being more respectful, or reflecting back to them what you've heard. You may get some strange looks. They'll get used to it and so should you, if you persevere.

As we mentioned in Chapter 1, Kouzes and Posner state that leadership is a conversation. And the relationships we build – socially and professionally – are built one conversation at a time. The perceptions others have of their conversations with us are powerfully shaped by how well and respectfully they feel we have listened to them.

That's the ears in the Face of Communication covered. The next chapter is the first of two chapters on the eyes of the model.

The **Top 10** Key Points ...

1. Listening is hard work for everybody.

2. Leadership is a conversation, and the personal and professional relationships we build are created one conversation at a time. How well we listen plays a key role in the quality of our conversations, our relationships, and our leadership.

3. Look for answers in your conversations. Asking questions of the speaker indicates that you're engaged with what they are saying and listening carefully in the conversation.

4. Information removal is the idea of postponing the conversation until you have removed the distractions you currently have in front of you.

5. Silence your voice and silence the voice in your head so you can create clear mental space for genuine listening.

6. Set yourself a target or purpose when you are listening to someone else. It helps considerably to give yourself a reason and focus for listening.

7. During a conversation, encourage the other person with verbal and nonverbal gestures.

8. Narrate refers to relating to the speaker. There are several ways to do this. One of the best ways to do this is to occasionally use the speaker's words.

9. In emotionally-charged interactions, it pays to be aware of and manage your own emotional reactions as best you can.

10. Listening well is actually about respect – for the other person, for the subject being discussed, and for yourself.

chapter 11

Using Your Eyes (Part 1): Three Perceptual Positions

Although our natural default position is seeing things through our own eyes, in conversations where there are differences of viewpoint, this is the least helpful perspective to assume.

Jane is a very successful professional who had been promoted to a senior management role, leading a team of other professionals and administrative staff. But while her professional skills were undoubted and highly regarded, her people management skills were not in the same league. Much to her chagrin, she found herself defending herself against accusations of poor management and even bullying behavior towards some of her staff. Jane was genuinely shocked that her behavior was being perceived so negatively and, she believed, unfairly. During a communication workshop she attended, Jane was made aware of the power of perceptions and how even well-intentioned behaviors can communicate unintended negative messages. Jane is, by her own admission, a focused and task-oriented individual. Those qualities undoubtedly enable her to get a lot done and get it done well. Those same strengths, however, often became limitations when interacting with her staff. For example, to keep interactions short and focused, Jane didn't have a chair on the other side of her desk. A stand-up meeting is a quick meeting, she reasoned, neglecting to consider how the staff member might feel about standing while she sat. She also tended to avoid small talk and avoided interrupting people by greeting them when she arrived at her office. Again, well-intentioned but perceived as cold, aloof, or disinterested. Jane consciously considered the perspectives of those who were having trouble working with her and made some small but deliberate shifts in her behavior – such as providing a chair next to her desk, occasionally moving out from behind the desk for a conversation, and deliberately greeting a few people each morning on her way to her office. These small but conscious responses had a powerful influence on others' perspectives and on her working relationships with them.

The eyes on the face of good communication represent the view or perspective we each bring to a conversation. This chapter looks at the perceptual positions people hold in a conversation. What do they see, or choose to see? What do they not see or choose not to see? The perception a person has of any situation has a significant impact on the quality and outcome of the conversation. For instance, when you have a conversation based only on your own perspective of an event, situation, or circumstance it will be a different conversation from viewing the situation through the eyes of the other person you are in conversation with. In fact, the two of you probably won't be having the same conversation. And both of those conversations will be different again if an objective or neutral third party shared their perspective. So, in this chapter we want to give you a useful framework to deliberately manage and if necessary alter your perceptual position in conversation. Changing your viewpoint changes the quality of the conversation. Although our natural default position is seeing things through our own eyes, in conversations where there are differences of viewpoint, this is the least helpful position to assume.

Perceptual positions is a simple yet powerful tool enabling a leader to move beyond their own perception of a situation and into a richer and more informative space. It is a framework developed by John Grinder, one of the co-founders of *Neuro-linguistic programming* (NLP), and co-author, Judith De Lozier. They published a book called *Turtles all the Way Down: Prerequisites to Personal Genius*.[1] ("Turtles all the way down" is an expression used to "explain" the myth that the world is supported on the back of a turtle – which in turn must be supported by another, larger turtle ... and humorously answering the inevitable question about what might be supporting the final turtle.)

The perceptual positions tool reminds us of the importance of understanding the other person's point-of-view in our professional and social interactions. Gaining a greater appreciation of a conflicting perspective is the first step to reconciling differences. Just as the saying from the book *To Kill a Mockingbird* goes: "you never really know a (person) until you stand in his or her shoes and walk around in them." But the perceptual positions model goes further than just putting yourself in the shoes of the other person. It also helps a leader to take yet another step and emotionally detach themselves from the dialogue of their own and the other person's perspectives so they can take on what can be termed the "helicopter view."

This is a vital ability for effective leaders, as a 2015 *McKinsey Quarterly* article highlighted. In researching what leadership skills most closely correlated with leadership success, the authors surveyed a list of 20 leadership traits amongst 189,000 people in 81 diverse organizations around the world:

> What we found was that leaders in organizations with high-quality leadership teams typically displayed 4 of the 20 possible types of behavior; these 4, indeed, explained 89 percent of the variance between strong and weak organizations in terms of leadership effectiveness ... Solving problems effectively ... Operating with a strong results orientation ... Seeking different perspectives ... Supporting others.[2]

While each of these four leadership behaviors requires effective conversations, two in particular highlight the need to be able to manage perceptual positions: solving problems effectively requires the ability to gather and analyze information to support decision-making, as well as to manage team disputes; and seeking different perspectives requires the ability to encourage ideas and manage biases.

In essence, perceptual positions is a dissociative technique that is used to take the emotional charge out of an interpersonal encounter and enable greater insight, creativity, and productivity. It puts individuals in a space that facilitates collaborative decision-making. The tool assists managers to think and act resourcefully in dilemmas that may otherwise seem challenging. The principle behind perceptual positions is the very simple idea of firstly, acknowledging your own position (the "first position") is only one perspective and is limited; secondly, intentionally acknowledging the other person's perspective and trying to understand it (the "second position"); and thirdly, shifting to a broader and more mutually inclusive perspective (the "third position"). It is doubtlessly more difficult to do than it sounds.

Consider this brief "first position" interaction between Jack and Tom:

"No you are completely wrong Jack," a defiant Tom points out. "You have got it all wrong!"

"If you look at the facts, Tom, you are in fact wrong," comes the challenge from Jack.

"We'll have to agree to disagree," comes Jack's resigned response.

This is a fairly typical type of interaction where two people each approach a situation from their own perspective. They are limited to looking at the situation through their own eyes. In these circumstances, it is often characteristic of both people to devote more energy to defending their perspective than trying to understand the alternative point-of-view.

However, the preparedness to see things from the other person's point-of-view is the basis for collaborative problem-solving. To work together effectively, Jack and Tom need to understand and appreciate each other's perspective on the matter-at-hand. In other words, they need to put themselves in the shoes of other person. In the context of workplace conversations, this willingness and capacity to change perception is particularly important in negotiations, interviewing, and building robust working relationships.

Again, consider the dialogue between Marcia and Jennifer:

"I don't want to speak at tomorrow's meeting Jennifer," protested Marcia.

"Marcia I disagree with you," started Jennifer. "This is a perfect opportunity to put our case. Can you explain to me why you don't want to speak at the meeting tomorrow? I need to understand why."

"Sure, I don't feel comfortable about speaking at the meeting tomorrow. I am sure I will alienate someone with my opinion on the matter and I am concerned that I will destroy some working relationships with some key people," Marcia explained. "We have a major project coming up and I need the support of the department to complete this on-time," she added.

"I see now. I didn't realize that your reluctance to speak at tomorrow's meeting was about that. I thought your reason was that you didn't think it was that important," came Jennifer's response.

"I do think it is important, Jennifer, but I also think that having good working relationships with the department is equally – if not more – important," said Marcia.

"Yes, I agree with you about that," replied Jennifer.

Jennifer opened the door to understanding Marcia's position by asking the question: "Can you explain to me why you don't want to speak at the meeting tomorrow? I need to understand why." Marcia's frank response helped Jennifer understand why she was reluctant to speak at the meeting. Jennifer assumed it was because Marcia didn't see the value in the opportunity. Although Jennifer's assumption was invalid, it nevertheless was her perception, making it her reality. And our perceptions often give rise to emotions like frustration, anger, and disappointment.

Having established this second position, a position of understanding, a leader can move to an even richer and broader perceptual position, third position. Third position offers an even more informative perspective than the combination of the second and first positions. In third position, the leader not only takes into consideration the other person's conflicting point-of-view, but also a range of external factors relevant to the conversation. Progression from first to second and then to third position expands the leader's vision or perspective. In the context of management conversations, the leader in third position is essentially taking on an organizational or systems perspective.

Consider this dialogue, a continuation of the conversation between Jennifer and Marcia:

"Okay, now that I understand your perspective on the matter of speaking at tomorrow's meeting, we need to think about how we can balance the need to maintain good working relationships with the department on the one hand and still get our message to those people clearly," strategized Jennifer. "Seeing as you are the project manager and need to work closely with these colleagues on the forthcoming project, it might be best for me to deliver that message. What do you think Marcia?"

"I think they will still be angry; but at least I will be able to continue working with them in the future," replied a partially relieved Marcia.

Third position does more than expand a leader's perspective. To be truly in third position, a leader has to remove themselves from the emotional clutch of defending their position on the one hand and/or attacking the conflicting position on the other hand. Whilst the leader may still feel strongly about their position on the matter, they can, at the same time, disassociate themselves from the feelings generated at the outset of the dialogue. Briefly, the leader in third position can see the differences in viewpoint in the context of a bigger picture.

Figure 11.1 illustrates the three significant perceptual positions.

Let's briefly explore each of these positions and their relevance for having constructive leadership conversations.

First position (*Self*)

First position, illustrated in the bottom left-hand side of Figure 11.1, is seeing things through our own eyes. It is the perceptual position most people are in most of the time, often subconsciously. In first position, we are viewing things purely from our own perspective. First position is your own perceptual position as you experience it and believe it to be as you look at the world through your own eyes, experiences, and beliefs. In NLP, this is referred to as a "fully associated" position; that is, you are wholly in it and living it as if it is happening now.

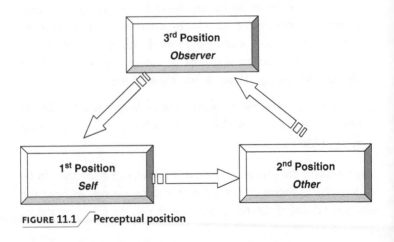

FIGURE 11.1 / Perceptual position

For example, two people arguing passionately with each other is a classic case of both parties adopting first position. Neither is listening to the other and both are defending their own point-of-view aggressively. This could possibly be accompanied by finger pointing, accusations, interrupting each other, and loud voices. You don't have to be in an argument to be in first position, but two people being in first position will often lead to an argument. Any time a manager is viewing a situation only through their own eyes they are limited to a first position perspective. It is the least helpful of the three positions in terms of being effective. Useful conversations don't occur when both parties are adopting a first position stance.

A constructive two-way conversation may very well start out with both people adopting a first position perspective. This is particularly the case when two people have strongly-held beliefs, opinions, or arguments about a matter. These differing positions may, for example, include differences in priorities, dissimilar perspectives about the outcome of a particular meeting, or contrasting methodologies for tackling a problem. Despite the limitations of each person's first position perspective, they nonetheless can provide a useful starting point for both parties to clearly and respectfully state their conflicting viewpoints. But whether the conversation is ultimately constructive will largely depend on the capacity of at least one person – and ideally both of them – to shift their perceptual position from first to second and ultimately to third position.

Second position (*Other*)

Second position, shown on the bottom right-hand side on Figure 11.1, occurs when a person puts themselves in the shoes of the other person. This position involves trying to understand the other person and their worldview. In second position, the person is looking through another person's eyes; acknowledging their different point-of-view. Of course, it is not possible to completely understand the other person or their perspective, but acknowledging, considering, and appreciating their perspective is feasible. To move to second position, a manager needs to listen without prejudice or judgment to the argument of the other person. This means momentarily suspending personal beliefs, prejudices, and values. It means remaining silent vocally and mentally while you attempt to see the other person's perspective. This is challenging to do, but necessary.

The second position is the perceptual position of an "other." It's about walking, seeing, hearing, feeling, and thinking from the perspective of the other person. This time you are looking through another person's eyes; appreciating the other person's point-of-view. This doesn't mean that you can't still hold your opinion (first position). It's not about agreeing with them or abandoning your perspective. You can still believe what you believe and you will still retain your own point-of-view. The difference is that in this second position you at least acknowledge – and hopefully begin to understand – the other person's perspective, assuming of course that it is different from your own. And sometimes by appreciating the other person's point-of-view, your perspective on the subject can adapt or at least be better informed.

Constructive conversations between two people with divergent views must move at the very least from first to second position. As a general rule, the longer two people stay in first position, the more protective they become of their point-of-view. To resolve a difference of view, you must first understand the other person's position. As the late Stephen Covey reminded us in *The 7 Habits of Highly Effective People*: "Seek first to understand, then to be understood."[3]

Consider the example earlier where two people were having an argument. If one of the two stops arguing for a moment and invites the other person to state their case and genuinely listens without prejudice, they are attempting to move from first to second position. As this person listens with interest to the arguments of the other person, they put themselves into a position to potentially gain a different perspective. At the very least, this person will gain a deeper insight into the other person's perspective. As we mentioned, they don't have to necessarily agree with the other person's point-of-view, just acknowledge it and seek to understand it.

Second position is being able to understand and empathize with the other person's position on a particular matter. Donna Blinston, an author on the subject of perceptual positions, makes the point:

> Being able to see things from another person's perspective enables you to understand what is important to them; knowing that, it helps you to empathize with them and communicate even more effectively as you will be respecting and relating to their values.[4]

Using open questions such as *Why* do you say that? *What* exactly do you mean? *How* does that affect you? And *how* did you arrive at that conclusion? encourages the other person to elaborate on their stance. Even closed questions like *Which* person are you referring to? *Where* did this take place? *When* did this take place? communicate a desire to understand their perspective and experience. The goal here is to understand and appreciate a different view from your own.

Third position (*Observer*)

Third position, as illustrated at the top of Figure 11.1, is a superior perceptual position to first and second position. In third position, you may still have your own opinion (first position), you also understand the other person's conflicting perspective (second position), but you now want to take a more objective view than either or both of those perspectives. In other words, you want to step back emotionally from the conversation and step up to a more dispassionate and objective viewpoint. Third position is a classic collaborative position, partly because it removes the sense of opposition or surrender that can arise from first or second position only perspectives.

Third position is a classic collaborative position, partly because it removes the sense of opposition or surrender that can arise from first or second position only perspectives.

The third position is outside the first two, but it suspends any beliefs or assumptions about both first and second positions. John Hoag refers to third position as "friendly visitor from outer space who has just arrived" perspective.[5] Third position is a synthesis of first and second positions as well as a third-party view. It is a position of problem-solving or collaboration. In this position you can look at the issue from the point-of-view of the team, organization, the industry, the market, the environment, or an even wider frame-of-reference.

In third position, you are interested but not directly involved; a neutral observer, someone who is removed or independent from your view and the other person's view. It's a useful position for gathering more information and balancing the task-at-hand with maintaining the working relationship.

Third position, as noted earlier, is like applying a helicopter view to the issue. You remove the emotions from the debate and invite the other party to work with you to resolve the dilemma. In third position, while encouraging the other person to work with you to resolve the matter, you keep in mind your position and their position within the context of relevant external factors that may impact on the issue.

Not seeing the forest for the trees or not seeing the trees for the forest?

Moving from first to third position is like observing a forest. First position is having your head up against a tree in the forest. Having your nose pressed up against a tree trunk, you cannot see the forest. All you can see is a single tree trunk at close range. Your worldview in this position is the tree trunk (first position). You step back from the tree and you discover there are other trees close by that are different in shape and size. You can now see that "your" tree is just one among many (second position). You then get into a helicopter and hover high above the forest. All you can see is a sea of green. But your knowledge of first and second positions helps you to understand that this sea of green is made up of thousands of individual trees. Your perspective has not simply changed, it has been enriched and transformed (third position).

Let's return to the example of an argument between two people. After successfully listening actively, at least one – and preferably both people – are now capable of understanding the other person's point-of-view. They then ask the other person to work with them to problem-solve, taking into account the opportunities and constraints they both face (external factors). This would be a case of shifting to third position.

Training yourself to move beyond first to second and ultimately to third position is fundamentally important in conversations where there are differences in point-of-view. It requires the ability to actively listen and genuinely engage with the other person. Indeed, one of the practical payoffs that comes from listening actively is the way it helps us construct both second and third positions.

Shifting perceptual positions seems like commonsense, but it is more difficult than it sounds. Most of us, most of the time, are looking at things through our own eyes, often without realizing it. Being conscious of the perceptual positions model can help jolt us out of this natural state. This can be particularly challenging when we are emotionally committed to a particular perspective. For example, if we hold a value of fairness and equity, we will naturally – and rightly – take a position that is consistent with these values. It may be difficult to suspend our beliefs temporarily so that we can hear another perspective. The important point here is that we don't have to give up our position. We just have to be willing to suspend it long enough and be open enough to acknowledge a different point-of-view.

Like the skills of enhancing your listening capabilities that we covered in the previous chapter, you can practice the skills of perceptual positions in the very next conversation you have. And we would urge you to do so while it is top of mind.

In the next chapter, we turn our attention to physical cues and behaviors in Part 2 of *using your eyes* in the Face of Communication.

The **Top 10** Key Points ...

 Perceptual positions is a simple yet powerful tool enabling a leader to move beyond their own limited perception of a situation.

2. Gaining a greater appreciation of a conflicting perspective is the first step to reconciling differences.

3. In essence, perceptual positions is a dissociative technique that is used to take the emotional charge out of an interpersonal encounter.

4. The principle behind perceptual positions is the very simple idea of firstly understanding the other person's perspective and then shifting to a broader, more mutually inclusive perspective.

5. First position is seeing things through our own eyes. It is the perceptual position most people are in most of the time, often subconsciously.

6. First position is your own perceptual position as you experience it, looking at the world through your own eyes and therefore not taking into consideration anyone else's point-of-view.

7. Second position occurs when a person puts themselves in the shoes of the other person. This position involves understanding the other person and their worldview.

8. In second position, the person is looking through another person's eyes; realizing their different point-of-view.

9. In third position you may still have your own opinion (first position), you understand the other person's conflicting perspective (second position), but you now want to take a more objective view.

10. This third position is outside the first two, but it suspends any beliefs or assumptions about both first and second positions.

chapter 12

Using Your Eyes (Part 2): Watching and Being Watched

We don't only listen with our ears. We can also listen with our eyes – watching for the important nonverbal messages that people are sending. And this also means that we are communicating – intentionally or otherwise – by the way we behave.

The first thing I noticed about Bruce was what I saw as he entered the room from the corridor. I'd been waiting for Bruce to arrive for our meeting. We'd met before, so I recognized Bruce straightaway. Recognizing him was instinctive. So was noticing him. And although I didn't consciously at the time "notice myself noticing him," what I did notice had an immediate influence on how I entered the conversation with Bruce. What I noticed was that Bruce was not noticing me. His head was buried in his phone. Even as he entered my "space" and encountered my outstretched arm, his eyes were still down, focused on a text-based message from someone else. Try as I might not to feel ignored, my emotional response was to feel offended and unimportant. As Bruce encountered my hand (now conveniently in his downcast eye-line) he broke his step, looked at my hand, looked up at me, forced a polite smile, and said "Hi." And then buried his head in his phone as he made his way to his seat. "Wow," whispered a colleague after I'd also sat down at the table. "Did you see that?" I'm guessing you had the same reaction as we did. And you probably also recognize that Bruce was unaware that the behavior everyone else in the room had observed had such an influence on our perception of him and his attitude towards us and our meeting.

The eyes in the Face of Communication model remind us that a critical component of communication exists outside our words. We don't only listen with our ears. We can also listen with our eyes – watching for the important nonverbal messages that people are sending – intentionally or otherwise. And this means we too are communicating – intentionally or otherwise – by the way we behave.

Our physical behaviors and actions communicate volumes beyond our words. Just as in the case of our friend Bruce above. The visual messages we send and receive frame our conversations before a word is uttered and stay with us after the conversation has turned silent. Because our brains are much more powerful image processors than they are word processors, the visual imagery that our behavior creates sends richer, faster, and potentially more powerful communication than our words will.

The visual messages we send and receive frame our conversations before a word is uttered and stay with us after the conversation has turned silent.

The work of Albert Mehrabian is often simplistically cited to illustrate this. In his 1967 book, *Silent Messages*, he suggested that 55 per cent of a message is in the nonverbal, 38 per cent in the tone of voice, and just 7 per cent in the words themselves.[1] This is often misrepresented to suggest that it doesn't matter what we say, what matters is how we communicate it nonverbally. Mehrabian's point, however, was actually about congruence – is there consistency between what we are saying (the words), the tone with which the words are said, and the physical behaviors accompanying the words? This really goes back to Aristotle, who talked about the importance of aligning the words, the voice, and the body.

Authentic conversation is "congruent" – there's alignment and consistency between our words, our tone, and our behavior. What this alignment does is allow our words to communicate, unhindered by distracting or conflicting visual or aural messages that may cause others to filter or block the language being used.

The eyes in our Face of Communication model tell us that we can learn much about the real meaning of what is being said to us by paying attention to the nonverbal aspects of another person's conversation with us. The eyes in the model also reinforce that our own messages will be more effective if we are aware of and able to manage our own behaviors. Carol Kinsey Goman, in her book, *The Silent Language of Leaders*, expresses this point well:

> Human beings are genetically programmed to look for nonverbal cues and to quickly understand their meaning ... Body language is in the eye of the beholder. The impact of your nonverbal communication lies in what others believe you intend and how that perception guides their reactions ... In a 30-minute negotiation, two people can send over eight hundred different nonverbal signals. If you focus on the verbal exchange alone and ignore the nonverbal element, you stand a high chance of coming away from that negotiation wondering why in the world your brilliantly constructed bargaining plan didn't work the way it was supposed to.[2]

But like a lot of things in communication, managing our behaviors is not as easy as it sounds for several reasons. One constraining factor is that we are often unaware of our behaviors when we are talking with others.

The meeting

At an executive team meeting, a group of senior leaders from a large organization were meeting to discuss current issues and planning strategies for the year ahead. Each had been asked to address their colleagues in turn. What struck one of the authors, who was facilitating the session, was the lack of awareness most of the executives had about their nonverbal behaviors at the table. When it was their turn to speak it was common to see them lean back, fold their arms, turn slightly away from the group, look down, or fail to engage in direct eye contact with each of their colleagues. With their permission, a video camera was quickly set up and the session recorded so that each of the executives could later see for themselves how their verbal messages were often being significantly compromised by distracting or misaligned body language. While viewing ourselves on video is rarely enjoyable, it does provide realistic feedback about how we are presenting ourselves and how others see and understand us through our behaviors.

Equally, we take for granted how powerful our visual impressions of others are when we are interpreting their communication. Again, this is because our brains are primarily image processors. And a major part of the visual processing our brains do is for the purpose of quickly classifying or categorizing what is happening so we know how to respond. Andrew O'Keefe, in *Hardwired Humans*, elaborates on this point:

It won't come as any surprise that we humans make quick judgments about people and situations. You've likely experienced what it's like to be judged too quickly and at other times you've no doubt been hasty in your own assessment of others. What might be news is the reason we make these quick judgments.

We do so in order to classify our experiences. Rather than engage in time-consuming analysis, we rely on first impressions and gut feelings to quickly classify people, situations and experiences ... Classifying is part of our survival machinery – to screen information into "good" and "bad" and other binary categories and to do so quickly.[3]

Daniel Kahneman explains this process in his book, *Thinking, Fast and Slow*. Kahneman's Nobel Prize winning work on judgment and decision-making covers more than 40 years, during which he worked with his late research partner, Amos Tversky, to understand better how the human mind works. He uses the terms "System 1" and "System 2" to describe the two modes of thinking that we use to process information and make judgments:

System 1 operates automatically and quickly, with little or no effort and no sense of voluntary control.

System 2 allocates attention to the effortful mental activities that demand it, including complex computations ...

When we think of ourselves, we identify with System 2, the conscious, reasoning self that has beliefs, makes choices, and decides what to think about and what to do. Although System 2 believes itself to be where the action is, the automatic System 1 is the hero of this book. I describe System 1 as effortlessly originating impressions and feelings that are the main sources of the explicit beliefs and deliberate choices of System 2 ...

System 1 continuously generates suggestions for System 2: impressions, intuitions, and feelings.[4]

This unconscious but powerful quick assessment of others is something we all do and something we all have done to us every day. As

Kahneman notes, this is not something that we can turn off, but we can learn to manage it and enable it to work more effectively for us. Awareness of this process is the first step and, in considering our own and others' nonverbal behavior, it is useful to think of the various elements and actions that are occurring within two broad dimensions that we might call the "physical" and the "symbolic."

Physical actions

Physical actions like gestures, posture, movement, eye contact, facial expression, and touch are all communicative behaviors that can express different things or be interpreted in different ways.

Gestures typically occur through the arms and hands. They give expression to our words and tone of voice. Small gestures – for example, from the wrist – tend to communicate uncertainty and timidity; large gestures tend to communicate confidence.

Gestures with the head are also important in communication. Think of the way an aggressive person will thrust their head forward, not back; how a timid or threatened person's head will retract into their shoulders (like a turtle). Or what the effect of a nod can be – either in acknowledgment of someone else's words or in silent support of your own assertions. How about the thrust jaw or the dropped neck, directing eyes at the floor? Or the slow, side-to-side shake of a head signaling disbelief versus the rapid shake of rejection. Or the slight tilt of the head to one side that silently says, "Tell me more." All of these gestures have meanings in and of themselves.

An absence of gesture is not necessarily negative, but it can reduce the impact of what we are saying. And forced or unnatural gestures create misalignment between words and actions – and the eye will note the disconnect.

Posture is about how we hold and move our bodies. Our posture is a powerful nonverbal signal we send. Do we look strong, open, controlled, and confident? Or is our posture closed, weak, and uncertain? Either way, it sends a signal we pick up easily and subconsciously.

Social psychologist, Amy Cuddy, from the Harvard Business School, has studied the effects of body language on hormone levels, feelings, and behavior. She has found that deliberately adopting more powerful, confident postures for as little as two minutes can improve testosterone and cortisol levels, helping our brains cope better with stressful situations.[5]

So our posture is not only sending signals to others, but to ourselves as well. Professor Erik Peper found that choosing to alter body posture to a more upright position can improve mood and energy levels. Peper postulates that:

> It may be possible that the decrease in physical activity and the increase in passive collapsed sitting and walking are factors that have contributed to a significant increase in depression over the last 50 years.[6]

No doubt part of the effects of tall and upright postures on confidence is the positive effect it has on breathing, with the steady rich flow of oxygen more effectively feeding the brain.

Movement in communication can be as subtle as a motion of the head or as dramatic as leaping from a seated position to standing in defiance of someone's comment. Rapid movement can communicate energy but it can also send signals of agitation, anxiety, and nervousness. Generally, power tends to be associated with and communicated by calmer and more deliberate movements. This is aided by a strong posture and correct, steady breathing, rather than the shallow, rapid breathing induced under stress.

Eye contact in Western cultures sends signals of respect and self-confidence. Looking at someone acknowledges their presence and opens up the lines of communication. Just like the Zulu greeting "*Sawu bona*," our eye contact says to someone "I see you." Because we tend to give higher status people more eye contact, looking at others while they are talking shows respect. Likewise, being able to hold another's gaze communicates confidence. (Staring, of course, sends a message of hostility – so it's important to manage eye contact within social conventions.) Sharing our eye contact in group settings enables everyone to feel acknowledged and accepted; focusing only on one or two persons suggests others aren't important and are not included in the conversation.

Facial expressions are possibly what we notice most in those with whom we are communicating. And yet we often fail to consider what messages our own facial expressions may be communicating. The raised eyebrows, the furrowed brow, the smile, the curled lip … you didn't need interpretations when you read those descriptions. They universally mean surprise or happiness, concentration or concern, acceptance or warmth, rejection or contempt. Our facial expressions can work for or against our messages, so they're worth analyzing (typically through video feedback from slightly stressful situations like meetings or presentations) to discover what unconscious signals we may be intentionally or unintentionally sending.

Touch is known as haptic communication, and can communicate everything from concern and comfort to domination and punishment. And before dismissing touch as inappropriate in professional settings, don't forget it is almost essential in everyday professional greetings and goodbyes through the handshake, and in some cases kissing on the cheek(s). The eyes, the ears, the voice, and the hands all combine at this point to make a potentially significant connection with another person.

Other types of touch can occur in professional settings as well: the guiding hand, the pat on the back, the comforting touch to a shoulder or forearm, the high-five, and more recently the fist bump. While advising "caution and good sense when using touch," Carol Kinsey Goman also advises professionals not to completely ignore the positive impact of touch in nonverbal communication:

> Whether it is a handshake, a congratulatory high-five, or a supportive pat on the back, touch can become an essential part of business communication. We are programmed to feel closer to someone who's touched us. The person who touches also feels more connected. It's a compelling force, and even momentary touching can create a human bond. A touch on the forearm that lasts a mere fortieth of a second can make the receiver not only feel better but also see the giver as being kinder and warmer.[7]

The use, interpretation, and appropriateness of touch varies widely from person to person and culture to culture, so it's important to be somewhat informed and aware of people's expectations before applying your own standards and communicating something entirely unintended! Nevertheless, physical touch and nonverbal communication are important, and often overlooked, aspects of the process of communication. How you are being observed and what you observe is a dimension of face-to-face conversations that should not – and cannot – be ignored.

Symbolic elements

Our physical actions communicate a range of messages that frame and influence how we are perceived and understood. So too, symbolic visual elements such as dress, artifacts, and environment can enhance or detract from the message we are trying to communicate or interpret.

Dress is a symbolic means of communication that is evident in organizational cultures. Think of the Wall Street lawyer or banker in a charcoal suit, cufflinks, and silk tie; the Seattle high-tech corporate type in jeans and a tee-shirt; the nurse, bus driver, or park ranger in their uniforms. Dress is a code that signals status, power, role, membership, and even culture.

"Dressing for success" is really about ensuring that how you dress enables your communication to be effective. Or at the very least, dressing suitably so that you minimize distractions or prevent confused signals between what is being said and what is being seen.

Artifacts are the things that we wear, use, and surround or associate ourselves with. They also communicate visual messages to others. Artifacts can be either intentional or unintentional cues that frame and convey positive or negative signals for interpretation. The office building. The sculpture and artwork in corporate foyers and lobbies. The corner office. The furnishings and décor in offices and meeting rooms. The crockery and glassware on the tables. The type of technology in use. The type of phone or tablet you use, your briefcase or bag, your watch, and jewelry – each of these are artifacts that are symbolic messages that provide visual associative cues. It is important to consider these and ensure they are congruent to the message being communicated.

The *environment* is another significant influence on the communication we engage in and it shapes the way we experience it. Are we invited to meet in a busy public café or invited into someone's office? Is our conversation in a private and quiet place or is it public and noisy? The formality or informality and the public or private settings can influence the dynamics of the conversation we are involved in.

How space is used is also an important environmental consideration. For instance, positioned across a desk and meeting "front-on" is a more adversarial arrangement. Picture, for example, management on one side of a board room table and union officials on the other side. This configuration is likely to be more confrontational. Alternatively, being positioned across a shared corner of a desk or meeting table, or side-by-side, or around a coffee table will tend to lead to a more collegial conversation. These are examples of how space and positioning can influence the environment for conversation.

AT THE SCREEN FACE ...

"Show me, don't just tell me"

The phrase "show me, don't just tell me" has long been used to remind writers – especially journalists – that communicating is about more than just facts and information. Writers try to create word pictures to help readers see more clearly what they are talking about. (It also reinforces that very old saying that "a picture paints a thousand words.") One of the great benefits of virtual communication is that it so often allows us to "show" others what we mean by sending them a photograph. From tradespeople taking photographs of a job site or parts, or someone considering buying a piece of equipment, to a team member on-site wanting to show their colleagues how a piece of equipment fits or works, the use of photos is enriching and speeding up the sharing of information in practical ways. Whether by email, Facebook, or collaboration sites like Yammer, adding a picture really can save a thousand words. Because when you show me rather than just tell me, I'm much more likely to say "I see!"

Like other aspects of nonverbal behavior, our physical and symbolic communication is on display every day. Symbolic communication can be intentional or unintentional, but it is "in play" nevertheless.

As communicators, it is vital we remember that we must both observe others' nonverbal messages and manage our own to ensure the clear understanding and insight that is central to effective professional conversations.

In this chapter, we have considered many of the elements beyond the words used that have an impact on the message we or others are trying to communicate. In particular we have looked at physical actions such as nonverbal communication and symbolic elements. It is important not only to be aware of our own message and the nonverbal dimension but also to be observant of the messages of others beyond the words they use. Briefly, we can listen with our eyes as well as our ears.

Chapter 13 looks at the power of questions on communication, symbolized by the nose?

The **Top 10** Key Points ...

1. Authentic conversation is "congruent" – there's alignment and consistency between our words, our tone, and our behavior.

2. Human beings are genetically programmed to look for nonverbal cues and to quickly understand their meaning. Body language is in the eye of the beholder.

3. Nonverbal communication includes both physical and symbolic elements.

4. Posture is about how we hold and move our bodies. Our posture is a powerful nonverbal signal we send. Physical movement in communication can be as subtle as a movement of the head or as dramatic as leaping from a seated position to stand in defiance of someone's comment.

5. Eye contact in Western cultures sends signals of respect and self confidence.

6. Facial expressions are possibly what we notice most in those with whom we are communicating.

7. Touch is known as haptic communication, and can communicate everything from concern and comfort to domination and punishment.

8. Dress is a symbolic means of communication that not only sends messages about personal style and taste, but also about organizational or industry culture.

9. Artifacts are the things that we wear, use, surround, or associate ourselves with as a means of communicating visual messages to others. Likewise, we use those symbols to help us interpret relationships, culture, status, and context.

10. Environment and how we use it is also a significant influence on the way communication is framed and the way we experience it.

The Art of Inquiry in Conversations

We hear a lot about learning organizations. But we miss a lot of learning when we focus only on providing answers rather than tapping into the power of questions.

Mel was concerned about the growing use of social media by his younger team members. It bothered him that they weren't focused enough on their projects. How much time were they wasting? And it further upset Mel that they constantly seemed to be talking about what their professional colleagues at other firms or in other industries were doing – while it was interesting, it just made their meetings more complicated and left him feeling a bit, well, out of touch and out of date.

At a workshop on communication skills, he volunteered to share this issue with a small group of trusted colleagues, including one or two who were younger than him, as a topic for trying out questioning skills in group problem-solving. He put his problem to the group: "How do I stop my staff from using social media at work?" The group then applied intentional questioning techniques, based on Dr Michael Marquardt's Action Learning approach – essentially, using questions to inquire, probe, and understand, and making statements only in response to questions.[1] What the process revealed to Mel (and others of his mindset) was that where he was seeing social media use only as a problem, others were experiencing its benefits. Like any other communication tool, it needed to be managed, but it offered many potential benefits to Mel's team, his organization, and to him as a senior manager. Through the focused discussion, Mel changed his problem question to: "How can I best manage our use of social media in the team?"

As mentioned earlier, the nose is depicted in the Face of Communication model by the upturned question mark used in Spanish at the start of a sentence that is a question. It's a great signposting device in the Spanish language.

A conversation without questions can be quickly reduced to a series of back-and-forth statements, a recitation of existing views, facts, or opinions. Questions add the vital ingredients of reflection, investigation, and integration. "In all affairs it's a healthy idea, now and then, to hang a question mark on things you have long taken for granted," said the British author and philosopher, Bertrand Russell. We explore the value of questions in this chapter.

Appropriate and timely questions are a tool for adding depth and perspective to a conversation. Questions move us beyond statements of fact or opinion. They redirect our contributions based on our reflections about specific aspects of the issue under discussion. The judicious use of questions help those in a conversation to investigate potential new or under-examined aspects of a topic or issue. We can therefore develop our appreciation of the matter at hand by taking a more systemic, holistic view.

The well-worn neural pathway associated with a topic may serve us well in certain situations. But like a freeway that quickly bypasses small towns, a predictable and overworked conversation structure can also bypass a lot of potentially valuable information about a subject being discussed.

Why don't we ask more questions?

Questions are essential to learning. Without a question, our brains will naturally tend to simply return to and rely on existing knowledge – knowledge which may have served us well in the past, but knowledge which may also be limited, outdated, or flawed. As we discussed in Chapter 1, part of the challenge of a technically trained manager is the expectation – imposed and assumed – that the critical thing is to have answers. Answering questions becomes more important than asking questions. Yet we would contend that the business of leadership is about *asking* questions, not *answering* them.

Dr Michael Marquardt is author of *Leading with Questions*, and Professor of Human Resource Development and International Affairs at George Washington University. He is also the President of the World Institute for Action Learning. Action learning emphasizes the role of questions in problem-solving and team development. Marquardt's contention is that:

> When we become leaders we feel that it is important for us to have answers rather than questions … The ability to ask questions goes hand in hand with the ability to learn. A learning organization is only possible if it has a culture that encourages questions … When people around us clamor for fast answers – sometimes any answer – we need to be able to resist the impulse to provide solutions and learn instead to ask questions.[2]

While asking questions sounds simple enough, it's worth considering some of the things that discourage us from regularly and intentionally applying this important communication tool in our interactions:

• The expectation that managers provide answers (as already discussed). This expectation is fuelled by a need to feel and be seen as being in control and knowledgeable. Holding this view of ourselves means missing golden opportunities to create spaces for fresh thinking, learning, and innovation.

- The certainty that can come from what is already known, versus the unknown. Human beings like certainty and find comfort in the status quo. What we already know provides us with a sense of security and confidence. Questions can disrupt this feeling of certainty.

- The corollary of this need for certainty is a fear of the unknown. Questions can unearth unknowns. What may happen if our question or someone else's question reveals that we don't know or that we need to change? Uncertainty plays on our natural insecurities.

- Many people who find themselves in management roles are more comfortable *telling* than *asking*. Telling is characterized as a feature of the decisive, take-charge, action-oriented type of personality. These kinds of traits are considered – at least in many parts of Western business culture – as ideal for assuming formal leadership roles. But the "learning zone" is usually one of some discomfort just outside the edges of our comfort zone. Questions test our comfort zone; they indicate a level of vulnerability that is somewhat uncomfortable. It takes that difficult but important combination of humility and confidence to go there.

- Some organizational cultures are more uncomfortable with questions than others. We identified, for instance, paramilitary and military organizations, with clearly defined hierarchies, as examples in Chapter 1 of cultures typically less comfortable with asking probing questions. In these cultures, team members are accustomed to being told what to do and to giving directions when in formal leadership roles. While giving and following orders is critical in much of the work such organizations do, it is not the only way in which they operate. At its worst, this type of culture might be described as "check your brains at the door" when you arrive at work. Unsurprisingly, such cultures tend to breed dependence and limited ownership; they are often based on the traditional employment relationship we discussed in Chapter 2.

- Asking questions can feel awkward and have the potential to create a sense of confusion. "Don't those in charge around here know what they're doing?", we might hear. That's a cultural reaction based on the traditional dependency model. Awkwardness and confusion are almost inevitable in the earliest stages of unfamiliar change and learning experiences. It's important to be prepared for that. The more familiar people become with questions the more comfortable they become with the process – and the more everyday learning and change can become part of everyday experience.

- Another barrier to asking questions is not knowing what sorts of questions to ask. Being able to ask good questions is a skill like most communication attributes. There's more to effective questioning than simply using open or closed questions. We'll look at the skills involved in questioning in a moment.

Without attempting to address each of the above challenges in any specific order, what follows are some practical principles and tools for incorporating effective questions into formal and informal conversations at work.

Stretch thinking

Thoughtful questions stretch our current thinking. As Oliver Wendell Holmes once stated: "a mind, once stretched by a new idea, never returns to its original dimensions." No organization can afford to simply maintain its existing mindsets if it is to respond to the changes and challenges it faces. Albert Einstein famously said that the problems we face cannot be solved with the same level of thinking we used in creating them. The answers we have may have served us well – and may continue to do so – but we'll only know when they are questioned.

It might be worthwhile to track and take note of the frequency with which questions are employed in your workplace. Consider the meetings you participate in and the conversations you are involved in. One of the disciplines of action learning is to apply the "rule" in collaborative, problem-solving conversations.[3] The rule is that statements can only be used in response to a specific question. This approach shifts the communication dynamic away from one where the most assertive or frequently repeated statement (or assumption) takes precedence. By applying the action learning rule just mentioned, questions become the dominant focal point in the conversation. This changes the dynamic to where the most intelligent question sparks insight or shines a light on knowledge creation. It encourages, stimulates, and celebrates learning.

Without questions, our brains will naturally revisit and rely on common knowledge. Nothing new is learned. Questions activate our search for responses. The process of looking for answers opens up potential pathways to new knowledge and understanding.

Without questions, our brains will naturally revisit and rely on common knowledge. Nothing new is learned.

Generating solutions

Questions are not in themselves a magic formula for unlocking learning and creating new knowledge. Some questions simply frame issues in such a narrow or prejudicial way that the only answer that can be given is the one that is wanted. "Is everyone familiar with how well our standard operating procedure is working?" is an example of this type of question. It's frustrating and manipulative and serves only to maintain the status quo.

But solutions-focused questions seek to move us forward. They create energy by shifting the emphasis from the problem to the solution. For example: "Can I challenge you to think of some other options open to us to resolve this problem?"

Here are some examples of questions (and answers) that could be considered for applying a solution-focused approach to learning conversations:

What's already working?

In the face of most problems there are elements that aren't problematic and it's important to acknowledge and reinforce those things and, where possible, leverage them. This type of question also helps allay fears that questions are only designed to change things and disturb the status quo.

What do we want?

We don't merely want to fix the problem. We want to understand what "fixed" looks like. What is the "ideal state"? These are more focused, deliberate, and constructive questions.

What can be stated simply?

What is needed are clear statements of purpose, need, and action, not vague or generic statements full of management-speak or complicated rationales.

What is available now?

A solutions-focused leader asks "What is in place that might be used?" They don't ask "What don't we have?" until they've established what's already in place that might be better utilized.

What immediate, small next steps can be taken?

Creating early momentum is important. A solution-focused leader is looking for quick and usually low-risk actions that will create energy and optimism.[4]

A focus on the solution is a different mindset to a problem focus.

Encouraging a systems view

We've heard a lot about "learning organizations" for the past 25 years. But we miss a lot of learning opportunities when the focus is only on providing quick-fix, standardized answers rather than tapping into the power of inquiry. In 1990, Peter Senge popularized the idea of "systems thinking" through his book, *The Fifth Discipline*.[5] Senge promoted the idea of the *learning organization* where employees are encouraged and enabled to see, understand, and contribute to the larger organizational system of which they are a part. As we continue to point out, questions are key in supporting such a learning environment. Incisive and timely questions seek to explore the larger systems of which teams, projects, and activities are a part. Asking questions is the primary role of managers and team leaders who are responsible for the development of processes and people. It is their responsibility to engage team members in intentional conversations that unlock learning, create knowledge, and expand horizons and opportunities.

Creating knowledge

The primary challenge of tapping into the knowledge and wisdom that exists in people working in teams and across the organization is concentrated effort and attention. Leaders need to engage in consistent inquiry to ensure valuable tacit knowledge is shared and that new knowledge can be created.

Individuals, teams, and organizations have a wealth of tacit knowledge. Tacit knowledge is "the stuff we just know" or know how to do. It's experience. It's knowledge that's become intuitive. Riding a bike or playing a piece of music are examples of tacit knowledge. They are things that become innate with practice and experience. In the workplace, we learn how things work, how to do things, we develop "work-arounds" for solving problems. Not everyone knows these things or even knows of them. There aren't formal processes or manuals to explain them (at least not in the way they are actually done). But tacit knowledge is accessible and important for getting results. That means that this knowledge is:

- Easy to take for granted, rather than valued.
- Easy to lose when someone leaves a role or an organization.
- Easy to overlook when we are trying to improve the way we do things.

Explicit knowledge, on the other hand, is the knowledge that has been captured, codified, and articulated. It can be stored, transmitted, and transferred to others. Explicit knowledge is accessible and can be understood outside individual experience and knowledge. It's the "official" way things are done, reported, measured, and evaluated. The more open and shared knowledge we have available and accessible, the more knowledge we have to share and work with in teams and organizations. So, the more widely obtainable the information, the better informed and equipped we are to coordinate our activities and adapt to changing circumstances.

Organizations and groups operate at this "official" level through the explicit knowledge they have access to. But organizational members' effectiveness is also enabled by the availability and sharing of tacit knowledge. Finding ways to capture and share the "unofficial" tacit knowledge held by individuals and teams improves processes and practices. Tacit knowledge also contributes to the creation of new knowledge for adapting and innovating.

Apart from the need for concentrated effort, another challenge is how to tap the reservoirs of tacit knowledge. How can it be made available to others? Once tacit knowledge is shared, how then can it be harnessed to create new knowledge? These questions can be resolved with a committed and methodical approach to creating knowledge.

Ikujiro Nonaka has offered a thought-provoking and practical approach in his *Socialization*, *Externalization*, *Combination*, *Internalization* (SECI) model.[6] SECI describes a "spiral" of learning to enable ongoing knowledge creation. In other words, SECI is a description of how to provide intentional focus on capturing, sharing, and developing knowledge. And you'll notice that at its heart it involves conversations.

To start with, Nonaka and Noboro Konno emphasize the importance of a "knowledge creating space." Space to create knowledge must be encouraged and provided; that is, a space that is physical, mental, and social. Socialization in SECI describes the need to get people together to share what they know and how they do things; in other words, their tacit knowledge. Obvious? Well, yes, but it doesn't happen unless leaders create the space, find the time, and offer their support and encouragement. Without this knowledge-sharing space, people don't always feel safe or responsible to offer their input or ask others questions.

Simply talking about things and sharing knowledge has value. But it's important to also capture the value of these conversations through the externalization (the E in SECI) of this knowledge. In other words, it is important to intentionally make this implicit knowledge explicit for future reference by more people. The externalization process is important for surfacing what is known and not (yet) known; testing hard knowledge against assumptions; and linking individual tacit knowledge with broader knowledge bases.

One of the ways explicit knowledge can be leveraged to create new knowledge is when it is shared and combined with other existing, explicit knowledge. This is systems thinking. This combination (C in SECI) of explicit knowledge bases encourages people to build connections and relationships between component parts of the organizational system. The impact of considering the interdependencies of organizational systems is increased productivity, new learning, and continuous improvement and innovation.

Working through the process of socializing, externalizing, and combining knowledge will undoubtedly generate some initial dislocation and discomfort. After all, as new processes are adopted and old ways abandoned, people are moving out of the comfort zone we spoke of before. At any rate, you know from your personal experience that learning includes periods of uncertainty, awkwardness, and sometimes confusion. Through all of this discomfort, there is eventually an internalization (the I in SECI) of new ways. This is the stage in our learning where we make the shift from *explicit* to *tacit*; it is just the way we do things. This transition is like the new employee who initially didn't recognize any of the organization's customers or understand their needs, but who progresses to the point of anticipating their needs and initiating formal and informal contact. Internalized knowledge forms the foundation for new experiences. If the knowledge spiral is encouraged by leaders, information can be better understood, developed, and shared.

This spiral of knowledge creation can occur anywhere within and outside the organization. It can take place between individuals, whether they are peers, managers and direct reports, or coaches and coachees. Knowledge creation can take place within and between teams and groups. It can occur within an individual's own development and learning activities. The larger the scope of the spiral, the greater the potential impact of the knowledge creation process.

The spiral of knowledge does occur incidentally. But to maximize its potential in organizations, leaders ought to intentionally focus on its creation. Questions are central to the process for sharing, exploring and expanding knowledge.

Building relationships

We covered in Chapter 7 the four key tasks in relationship-building conversations: showing up, listening up, speaking up, and lifting up. Questions illustrate that we're present and engaged with the conversation; they prompt others to talk so we can listen to them; they are a means of speaking up without simply being declamatory; and they communicate our interest in and sense of value for others and their opinions. Questions build relationships.

Questions are the not-so-secret technique of those we know to be "good conversationalists." Good conversationalists put the focus on the other person so that they feel good about being in the conversation and feel respected and valued.

Whether you want to build a relationship, build intellectual capacity, build and share knowledge, or build a stronger team, the upturned question mark in our Face of Communication model is the reminder to regularly use questions in your conversations.

In the final chapter, we discuss how to create and maintain safe, open feedback channels.

The **Top 10** Key Points …

1. A conversation without questions is simply a back-and-forth exchange of statements.

2. Questions introduce greater sophistication to our conversations because they invite reflection, integration, and investigation.

3. Knowledge creation and organizational learning depend upon a culture of questions so that assumptions are challenged, ideas are explored, and tacit wisdom can be made explicit.

4. Asking questions requires self-discipline because of the implicit pressure leaders particularly face to provide answers. The desire for certainty and control can be a powerful barrier to inquiry.

5. The use of questions is linked to the communication culture we work in. If questions are viewed as conveying weakness, lack of authority, or hesitation then they will go unasked.

6. Questions stretch our thinking beyond familiar patterns and connections. Without them we conveniently and consistently return to the already-known.

7. There are different types of questions and each can help us more deeply or broadly gain insight when we learn how to use them skillfully.

8. Questions can help us frame issues under discussion, including orienting people to a solution-focused (rather than problem-focused) approach.

9. Systems thinking relies upon the ability to ask good questions that take into account broader perspectives and connections that influence the issues under discussion.

10. Relationship building through conversations is enabled and enriched by the quality of our questions and the interest they convey.

chapter 14

Creating and Maintaining Safe, Open Feedback Channels

Are you or your organization maintaining an "edge" by ensuring the two-way flow of communication? Or are you paying "ignorance tax"?[1] To stay connected to your operating environment and to tap into a team's intelligence requires a commitment to creating safe, open channels of honest, immediate information.

When Cam was asked in a coaching session about how often he had intentional developmental or feedback conversations with his top-performing team members, he initially tried to brush the question aside. "Not often," he said. "I don't need to. I let them get on with it." Still, asked the coach, how often? Visibly disturbed by the question now, Cam reiterated that he didn't see the need, so he "stayed out of their way, I delegate and I'm here if they need me." "So," the coach probed, when was the last time you had a deliberate, focused conversation about performance or ideas with one of your top performers?" Silence. Then a slow shake of the head. "I can't remember," Cam said. He now looked a bit distressed. "What are you thinking?" asked the coach. "This is potentially very dangerous," Cam said. "Any one of them could walk out the door tomorrow and I wouldn't see it coming. I couldn't replace them or the knowledge they'd take with them. I've left myself completely in the dark."

Communication is often referred to as the lifeblood of organizations. The free flow of vital information – up, down, across, out of, and into teams and organizations is what enables them to function productively and to continually improve and innovate. The absence of such communication flows causes confusion, frustration, wasted effort, mistrust, and stagnation. Like the flow of blood through a physical body, the continual, healthy two-way flow of communication in relationships, teams, and organizations is what keeps them alive, functioning, and vibrant.

The conversations that are taking place within, around, and about our relationships, our teams, and our organizations are central to their health and vitality. They're crucial vehicles for communicating. But those conversations are also valuable guides to the types and quality of our feedback systems.

The smiling mouth shape in our Face of Communication model reminds us of the feedback process shown in Figure 14.1. It typically shows a message being encoded by a sender to be transmitted via a medium or channel to a receiver who then decodes the received message and, ideally, responds with feedback related to the message. (This model is based on Shannon and Weaver's 1948 depiction of communication. While there are many more dynamic elements and influences in the human communication process, the model has formed a basis for understanding the elemental processes.)[2]

The communication flow model introduces some of the complexities of communicating and receiving a simple message. Further, it shows the potential barriers and breakdowns that can interfere in the flow of communication, and the fact that communication is an interactive and iterative process, not a controlled one-way event. For its effectiveness, the communication process is heavily reliant on the two-way interaction of the parties involved.

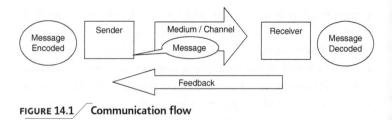

FIGURE 14.1 Communication flow

The difference between information and communication

Although we quickly recognize the various elements in such communication models, it's easy to ignore their reality in day-to-day conversations. This is why so often *information* is mistaken for *communication*. We live and work in environments frequently characterized by "information overload." Consequently, we spend a lot of time filtering out messages because there are just too many that we are somehow expected to respond to. So it's a mistake to assume that when we've sent information out, we have communicated. One useful way to differentiate is to think of *information* as being what we "push out," while *communication* is what others "take in." Communication is not what we say or send, but what others hear and understand. Which is why it's referred to as "meaning-making process." And we all know there can be a world of difference between what we meant to say and what someone else thinks we meant!

So the feedback element – the smiling mouth on our face of communication – is a vital tool for us to use if we're going to ensure our information is actually communicated. It enables us to ensure the message has got through and that it's been understood (and hopefully acted upon in the appropriate way).

But of course the feedback channel has much more to offer as well:

• It's a vital monitoring system to retain environmental awareness.
• It's an intelligence-gathering instrument.
• It's a relationship maintenance tool.
• It's a knowledge creation device.

However, as vital as our feedback channels are, they do not work automatically or by default. In fact, they need our active involvement and preservation to ensure their effective operation. Consider some of the things that prevent, block, or divert feedback in organizations:

• Absence of channels. The old "my door is always open" is a fool's self-deception that anyone can provide feedback anytime (for a start, see "power imbalance" and "danger" below).
• Lack of awareness of channels for giving feedback.
• Power imbalance (see Chapter 2).
• Gatekeepers who filter information.
• Perceived dangers or threats of providing feedback.
• Difficulty accessing channels.

Information flow "down" the organizational structure is not easy, but it's "a piece of cake" compared with getting information back "up" the organization, particularly in an organization based on the traditional psychological contract. Gravity, if nothing else, will ensure top-down messages find their way down the lines of reporting in some form. But getting information from the frontlines of the business back up to higher levels doesn't exactly have gravity working for it; that process is going to take some serious engineering.

lines of reporting in some form. But getting information from the frontlines of the business back up to higher levels doesn't exactly have gravity working for it; that process is going to take some serious engineering. Active "pull" mechanisms need to be intentionally established, primed, and supported. The slightest barrier – such as denial, criticism, or cautionary advice like "management won't want to hear about that" – is likely to quickly dry up the upward flow of information.

Creating and maintaining safe, open feedback channels is work that must be done at the interpersonal, team, and organizational levels. It's an everyday management and supervisory function.

AT THE SCREEN FACE ...

From little tweets, big conversations (and changes) grow ...

UK National Health Service (NHS) Improvement Leader, Helen Bevan, delivered a seminar presentation challenging the audience to identify ways to get commitments for change from others. Stuart Sutton, a GP, tweeted her following the seminar and so began a process that quickly culminated in the first NHS Change Day in 2013. The event generated 189,000 pledges from staff related to taking responsibility for positive organizational changes. They ranged from commitments to smiling more, to giving daily positive feedback to colleagues, to adapting a clinical simulation unit for nursing students to become patients for a day, to a chief executive spending time working as a nurse in a ward for elderly care.

NHS Change Day is a classic example of how widespread change can be instigated and mobilized "bottom-up," harnessing knowledge and energy.[3]

The edge

While the idea of sharing knowledge is obvious, its practice is frequently anything but, leading to what Gary Hamel calls organizational "ignorance tax":

> A little more humility at the top, and a lot more bottom-up knowledge aggregation, could substantially reduce the ignorance tax *your* company has to pay.[4]

Are you or your organization maintaining an "edge" by ensuring the two-way flow of communication? Or are you paying "ignorance tax"? To stay connected to your operating environment and to tap into a team's intelligence requires a commitment to creating safe, open channels of honest, immediate information.

Hamel identifies the task of "aggregating collective wisdom," and it is one of six twenty-first century management challenges he addresses in *The Future of Management* (2007).[5]

But one thing everyone knows intuitively about upward communication in organizations is that it's risky. Most employees have seen the messenger get shot for sharing bad news – or heard about the shooting! So we learn to be careful about what information gets passed "up." Sanitized, superficially supportive feedback from the frontlines tends to make life go more smoothly. But if information is being withheld, or distorted, assumptions take its place, questions aren't being asked, and trouble starts. Losing touch with reality, missing out on important information, and failing to acknowledge changing circumstances are organizational weaknesses that will certainly cost you an edge.

As much as we talk about flattened hierarchies, the reality is that organizations always have clear, implicit power structures. These power structures usually have clear lines of authority and convey unspoken messages about "who knows best" and "what's right." Challenging the status quo – even with the best of intentions – is typically seen as an irritation or interruption at best, subversive and destabilizing at worst. The price of this safe, upward communication is what Hamel refers to as ignorance tax that leaders impose on themselves and their teams and organizations.

It is the "richness" – not just volume, but value – of information that flows in a team and an organization that creates advantages, flexibility, and insight. This is the edge. But that flow of information depends upon the accessibility and safety of communication channels. These channels are characteristic of the culture we outlined in Chapter 3, illustrated in the new employment relationship model.

In his book, *The New Leaders*, Daniel Goleman, who popularized the concept of emotional intelligence, writes about what he calls "CEO disease." CEO disease is "the information vacuum around a leader created when people withhold important (and usually unpleasant) information."[6] Of course this doesn't happen only to CEOs. Nor is it only an "upward" communication problem. Employees are often unintentionally deprived of the organization-sustaining lifeblood of accurate, up-to-date information too. So why does this happen? And how can we open up the flow of accurate, timely, and relevant information?

Communication channels

The first question to ask is whether there is an accessible means of transmitting information, feedback, concerns, and ideas upwards? Providing these communication channels is a fundamental responsibility of leadership. Communication has to flow through channels – formal and informal. It's easy to assume this is the case, but how exactly does information flow?

Questions that need to be considered by organizational leaders are:

- Are there communication channels in place?
- Are they open?
- Who are they open or closed to, intentionally or accidentally?
- Are they accessible?
- Who are they accessible to; for example, what about people outside major centers, or those for whom internet access is limited?
- Are people actively encouraged to use feedback channels?
- Are contributions responded to quickly and honestly?

In the past, information was controlled by those with power and status. The age of social media has destroyed that idea. But organizational thinking and processes often still default to assumptions of control. Resistance may be a short-term replacement for control but it will, ultimately, prove futile.

But even if communication channels are in place, are they safe to use? The safety factor will ultimately make or break the quality of the dialogue. If people feel secure using an avenue of communication, then interaction will increase and the information given will be more in-depth. This leads to added value to discussions, decisions, and direction. If, on the other hand, the channel is not safe or trusted, then the information flow will be limited and lean. This leads to an impoverished environment for meaningful conversation. A lack of safety means unpleasant, unwanted, or unexpected messages or questions are withheld. This ultimately starves everyone of the organizational "lifeblood" that creates the edge needed to survive and thrive.

We've all heard the age-old response to communication channels and safety: "My door is always open ... my people know they can tell me anything." Maybe. But it might be worth considering when the last time was that an employee shared anything hard, bad, sensitive, challenging, or disruptive to a senior manager in your organization? No news may not necessarily be good news. And if and when negative information is expressed, what is the response? The reaction from the manager will determine whether vital but unpleasant information is shared in the same way again, if at all. The person who needs to know may in future be left to suffer in silent ignorance.

As mentioned, it is ultimately the leader's responsibility to create and maintain safe and open channels for rich communication to flow in both directions. More specifically, to do this there needs to be two-way feedback and interaction, a balanced exchange of viewpoints, and open dialogue (which literally means "through words").

Promoting non-threatening dialogue

Further, we would like to suggest a three-stage process essential for generating and upholding non-threatening dialogue.

Model information sharing

The first step in this process is for leaders to *model information sharing*. People trust what they see. Our behavior is our most powerful communication tool. What we do carries more weight than what we say. Our behavior is more persuasive than any speech, meeting, or policy.

An important aspect of modeling information sharing is for leaders, with all their time pressures, to value informal channels of communication. Informal communication occasions are opportune and important times for feedback. They are often underrated and neglected episodes. Casual opportunities for feedback are undervalued and formal channels, such as the performance review, overvalued. Furthermore, informal channels are often more relaxed and trustworthy environments for open communication. This is particularly the case when the formal sessions are perfunctory affairs. Modeling information sharing also means promoting and seeking out informal feedback channels of communication. Looking for informal opportunities to seek and give feedback sets the tone from the leader.

Inviting upward feedback

Actively and genuinely *inviting upward feedback* is a second important step in cultivating and maintaining non-threatening dialogue. This is essentially done by asking questions that invite truth, observations, concerns, and ideas. By asking, the leader is demonstrating that they are interested. The late Peter Drucker said this was one of a leader's most valuable and yet under-used tools: asking "what must be done?" It is particularly important to seek feedback from those on the often forgotten frontline, who are usually closest to the customer and to changes in the operating environment.

Listening actively to the feedback

Inviting feedback is one thing, but *listening actively to the feedback* is the third important ingredient in this process of promoting non-threatening dialogue. That means listening all the way through the information, even if we think we've heard it all before. We may have heard this opinion expressed before, but maybe the employee hasn't talked it all the way through before. Or maybe they haven't been heard all the way through before. (Or maybe you haven't actually listened before! Why are you hearing this again and again …?) We have all been on the receiving end of this unpleasant experience, when our opinion and ideas have been dismissed before we finish our point. Ask questions. Really listen. It's not complicated. But it can give you or the team the edge.

And if you think this is just a waste of time, consider the effect if you just brush the person aside because you've heard it all before. They're not likely to share with you in the future when they have something you haven't heard before. Your time and attention is an investment.

Enabling this process to work requires attention to "safety." Every workplace has safety protocols, processes, and principles. We tend to think of safety in terms of physical operating environments, especially those involving machinery and equipment. But there's another sort of workplace safety that we too easily ignore.

We all know about the instinctive "fight or flight" response our brains have, but the effect of this response on the way people work together, how they contribute, and how they interact with those in leadership roles is often underestimated.

The "minimize danger and maximize reward" principle is central to how our brain organizes itself. The practical result in workplace interactions is what leadership coach, Dr David Rock, describes as an "approach-avoid" response. Rock explains that our brains "tag" various situations for easy reference:

> If a stimulus is associated with positive emotions or rewards, it will likely lead to an "approach" response; if it is associated with negative emotions or punishments, it will likely lead to an "avoid" response.[7]

Not surprisingly, these responses have implications for how we engage with other people, with problems, and with our leaders. As we learn more about how the brain works and how this shapes our interactions, it becomes increasingly apparent that managing our behaviors intelligently is essential. It is critical to getting the best out of ourselves and those who work with us by ensuring communication channels are open and safe.

When someone feels threatened, or even unappreciated or disrespected, they are much more likely to withdraw from the person or situation. This is a simple reflection of the fact that when we feel threatened or negative "resources available for overall executive functions in the prefrontal cortex decrease," explains Rock.

Clearly, such "avoid" responses are not helpful for maintaining the feedback systems that fuel creativity, collaboration, and innovation. Rock points out that "this response is the default situation that often occurs in teams." Because we are naturally more attuned to threats than rewards, "the threat response is often just below the surface and easily triggered. Just speaking to one's supervisor, or someone of higher status is likely to activate this response."[8]

AT THE COAL FACE...

You can feel the atmosphere in companies...

In our work with organizations large and small around the world, both of us have experienced the obvious "atmosphere" that is quickly detectable in teams and organizations. Those atmospheres can be detected in environments in which clients and staff speak glowingly about the organization, its work and, importantly, its people; where colleagues openly praise performance; where people at all levels express trust, appreciation, and confidence in each other; "safe/approach" environments, in other words.

And of course, it's just as easy to notice the other atmospheres of distrust, frustration, disrespect, and fear.

Human performance expert, Dr Adam Fraser, wrote about his assessment of companies he worked with that created healthy atmospheres: "What all these companies have in common was that the leaders did not see themselves as better than or above the other people in the business. They mixed with and were part of the broader team. The result was that these organizations were performing well, had very high engagement levels and had very low turnover of staff. All this saved them huge dollars and kept their culture alive. In contrast I have worked in other organizations where the leaders viewed the other people in the business with contempt and inferior to them. Funnily enough their engagement levels were lower and staff turnover much higher."[9]

From a leadership perspective, if our presence or our response to information creates an "avoid" reaction due to fear, uncertainty, or negative emotions or expectations, we won't be encouraging further sharing of intelligence. Rather, people will retreat into "safe" mode, focused on reducing risk and maintaining safety.

Now none of us, of course, consciously tries to stimulate that "avoid" response in others, but it's obvious when someone does it to us! That is, someone from whom we mentally, emotionally, or physically withdraw, or from whom we withhold information, or simply disengage. It may be fear, a lack of trust, uncertainty about intentions, or just the fact that this person is in a superior or more powerful position. Whatever the motive, our instinctive protective mode causes us to close down protectively rather than open up creatively.

It's common for those in the more powerful position to be oblivious to the potential for this "avoid" reaction. It takes consciously positive, sensitive, and reassuring behaviors to encourage an "approach" response when there's a power disparity.

A few years ago, Google decided to find out what separated the best and worst bosses in their organization. It turned out that technical expertise ranked dead last among the predictors of a boss's effectiveness. Instead, as *The New York Times* reported:

> What employees valued most were even-keeled bosses who made time for one-on-one meetings, who helped people puzzle through problems by asking questions, not dictating answers, and who took an interest in employees' lives and careers.[10]

Daniel Goleman and Richard Boyatzis, in an article reinforcing the "biology of leadership," state that:

> Leading effectively is … less about mastering situations – or even mastering social skill sets – than about developing a genuine interest in and talent for fostering positive feelings in the people whose cooperation and support you need.[11]

Again, we are reminded that the conversations we initiate and contribute to as leaders every day – the formal and the informal, the planned and the spontaneous – are central to the climate and culture of our teams and organizations. Goleman and others talk about the "emotional contagion" we experience in our teams and organizations, and the influence leaders have on the emotional climate. "Mood" is a powerful everyday force in our workplaces. According to Goleman and Boyatzis, "Being in a good mood, other research finds, helps people take in information effectively and respond nimbly and creatively."[12]

Our conversations are the day-to-day experiences people have of each other. Formal or informal, long or short, detailed or general, they shape our sense of safety, our moods, and our energy. As information sharing and information gathering vehicles, our conversational interactions have enormous potential. The crux is whether they invite feedback and sharing, or whether they warn people to avoid awkward but important issues.

Creating the safety that's required for communication to flow smoothly in both directions begins with the simple – but surprisingly challenging – quality of being approachable. It starts with a realistic self-awareness. This appreciation of how we are perceived by others results in making necessary adjustments in behavior. In practice, it means managing our behaviors and interactions with others in ways that communicate "safety" and "reward." Being sensitive to how others see us and making a genuine effort to be approachable are essential to encouraging others to contribute their best.

This principle of "approachability" is not soft or fuzzy. It's an attribute for communicating effectively in our increasingly complex operating environments. More and more, we are required to take a systemic view of our own work, that of our teams, our organizations, and even the industries or sectors we operate in. The knowledge economy is a complex web of communication that doesn't permit us to work in isolation. So the conversations we engage in traverse multiple realities and experiences. To do this effectively, we need to actively encourage real-time, real-world feedback from myriad sources. Conversations are the mechanism for the thinking, sharing, and experimenting necessary to react to the opportunities and challenges we face. This capacity is what we want. It's what we need. It's what we get if we intentionally and continuously create and maintain safe, open feedback channels.

In Summary ...

This brings us to the end of Part III and the book. It is timely to briefly recap on the terrain we have covered.

In Part I, we discussed the kind of culture necessary for fostering meaningful conversations. A culture that promotes constructive conversation is one based on a new psychological contract between employer and employee; one that is diametrically opposite from the traditional employment relationship of "them and us." In our view, culture is the most significant potential carrier or barrier to promoting great interactions in the changing workplace. But we identified nine other barriers that inhibit the potential for meaningful conversation.

In Part II, we defined and discussed the types of conversations that we believe are critical for individual, team, and organizational success. Briefly, we categorized these as conversations for development, conversations for building relationships, and conversations for making and reviewing decisions.

Part III covered the skills of conversations, illustrated by our model of the Face of Communication. Briefly, we explored the value and importance of active listening; our perceptual position in conversations and their impact on the quality of conversation; the significance of nonverbal language and symbols on the quality of dialogue; the use of questions as a tool of conversation; and finally, in this chapter, the importance of creating a safe and open environment for feedback to take place.

We wish you well with your conversations and your continuing leadership journey.

The **Top 10** Key Points ...

 Open, two-way flows of communication are the lifeblood of organizations.

There's a difference between "information" and "communication": information is what gets sent out; communication is what gets taken in. It's a participative, two-way, meaning-making process, not simply transmission of information.

3. Feedback channels are vital monitoring systems to maintain environmental awareness. They are intelligence gathering instruments, relationship maintenance tools, and knowledge creation devices.

4. Feedback channels are rendered ineffective if they are absent, but also if there are perceptions of power imbalance, gatekeepers who filter information, threats or dangers in providing feedback, or difficulty accessing channels.

5. Leaders who want to create effective, safe, open feedback channels must model information sharing themselves, because people trust what they see more than words or policies.

6. Leaders who want to create effective, safe, open feedback channels must actively invite upward communication – the good, the bad, and the awkward.

7. Leaders who want to create effective, safe, open feedback channels must listen attentively – even when they think they've heard it all before, because the person sharing the information may not have been heard before and you need to reassure them their input matters, so that they will be willing to talk to you again when they have something you haven't heard before.

8. The human "fight or flight" response presents itself in workplace communication as "approach or avoid," depending how safe people feel about sharing information.

9. Engaging effectively with others is largely dependent upon our willingness and ability to express genuine interest in what they have to offer.

10. Creating and maintaining safe, open feedback channels is critical to our ability to support systems thinking and approaches that enable real-time, real-world responses to the opportunities and challenges we encounter.

Notes

Introduction

1. P. Senge (1990) *The Fifth Discipline* (New York: Doubleday).

1 Organizations are Conversations

1. G. Bateson (1972) *Steps to an Ecology of Mind* (Chicago, IL: University of Chicago Press).
2. M. Simon (2013) "Driving workplace performance through high-quality conversations," *Strategic HR Review*, 13(1).
3. ibid.
4. http://www.therightconversation.co.uk/.
5. J. M. Kouzes and B. Z. Posner (2011) *Credibility: How Leaders Gain and Lose It* (San Francisco, CA: Jossey Bass).
6. http://www.therightconversation.co.uk/.
7. J. McCann (2014) *Talk is (Not!) Cheap* (New York: Harcourt).
8. R. F. Bowman (2002) "The Real Work of Department Chair," *The Clearing House*, 75(3), pp. 158–62.
9. J. K. Barge (2013) "Pivotal leadership and the art of conversation," *Leadership*, 10(1), pp. 56–78.
10. M. Silverman, E. Bakhshalian and L. Hillman (2013) "Social media and employee voice," March (London: CIPD).
11. Barge (2013) "Pivotal leadership."
12. http://www.therightconversation.co.uk/.
13. http://www.therightconversation.co.uk/.

2 The "Them and Us" Employment Relationship: A Culture of Discouraging Conversations

1. T. B. Baker (2014) *Attracting and Retaining Talent: Becoming an Employer of Choice* (London: Palgrave Macmillan).
2. This research is based on Baker's doctoral thesis, entitled: "Towards a new employment relationship model: Merging the changing needs and interests of individual and organisation." http://eprints.qut.edu.au/16064/.

3 A New Employment Relationship: A Culture of Encouraging Conversations

1. K. Weick (2009) *Making Sense of the Organization: Volume 2: The Impermanent Organization* (Chichester: John Wiley & Sons).
2. T. B. Baker (2009) *The 8 Values of Highly Productive Companies: Creating Wealth from a New Employment Relationship* (Brisbane: Australian Academic Press).
3. T. Mullaney (2012) "Social media is reinventing how business is done," *USA Today*, 16 May. http://usatoday30.usatoday.com/money/economy/story/2012-05-14/social-media-economy-companies/55029088/1.

4 The Nine Common Barriers to Communication

1. J. Dutton (2003) *Energize your Workplace* (San Francisco, CA: Jossey-Bass).
2. W. Bennis (1993) *An Invented Life: Reflections on Leadership and Change* (Reading, MA: Basic Books).
3. G. Hamel (2007) *The Future of Management* (Boston, MA: Harvard Business School Press).
4. M. Marquardt (2005) *Leading with Questions* (San Francisco, CA: Jossey-Bass).

5. National Transportation Safety Board (2006) *AirVenture Oshkosh 2006 Ed.*, 4th ed., Safety Report SR-06/01, Washington, DC.
6. National Transportation Safety Board Bureau of Accident Investigation (1978) "Aircraft accident report: United Airlines Inc., McDonnell Douglas-8-61," N808N2U, Washington, DC.
7. M. Chui, J. Manyika, J. Bughin, R. Dobbs, C. Roxburgh, H. Sarrazin, G. Sands, and M. Westergren (2012) "The social economy: unlocking value and productivity through social technologies," McKinsey Global Institute. http://www.mckinsey.com/insights/high_tech_telecoms_internet/the_social_economy.

5 Development Conversations: The Five Conversations Framework

1. T. B. Baker (2013) *The End of the Performance Review: A New Approach to Appraising Employee Performance* (London: Palgrave Macmillan).
2. ibid.
3. T. Rath (2007) *Strengths Finder 2.0.* (New York: Gallup).
4. A. Clarke, http://www.trainingjournal.com/blog/the-fiveconversations/.
5. For more information about non-job roles, see T. B. Baker, *The End of the Performance Review*.

6 Development Conversations: Five More Conversations

1. T. B. Baker (2013) *The End of the Performance Review: A New Approach to Appraising Employee Performance* (London: Palgrave Macmillan).
2. J. Greene and A. M. Grant (2003) *Solution-Focused Coaching: Managing People in a Complex World* (Harlow: Pearson).
3. D. Pink (2011) *Drive: The Surprising Truth About What Motivates Us* (New York: Riverhead).
4. J. Kouzes and B. Posner (2007) *The Leadership Challenge*, 4th ed., (San Francisco, CA Jossey-Bass).

5. S. Sinek (2011) *Start with Why: How Great Leaders Inspire Everyone to Take Action* (London: Penguin).

6. T. B. Baker (2015) *The New Influencing Toolkit: Capabilities to Communicate with Influence* (London: Palgrave Macmillan).

7. J. Kouzes and B. Posner (2009) "To lead, create a shared vision," *Harvard Business Review*, January. http://hbr.org/2009/01/to-lead-create-a-shared-vision/ar/1.

8. R. Goffee and G. Jones (2006) *Why Should Anyone Be Led by You?* (Boston, MA: Harvard Business School Press).

9. ibid.

10. D. Ulrich and W. Ulrich (2010) *The Why of Work* (London: McGraw-Hill).

7   Conversations for Building Relationships

1. L. A. DeChurch, J. R. Mesmer-Magnus, and D. Doty (2013) "Moving beyond relationship and task conflict: Toward a process-state perspective," *Journal of Applied Psychology*, 98(4), pp. 559–78.

2. ibid.

3. Edelman (2014) "2014 Edelman Trust Barometer." http://www.edelman.com.

4. S. M. R. Covey and R. R. Merrill (2006) *The Speed of Trust: The One Thing that Changes Everything* (New York: Free Press).

5. http://www.psychologytoday.com/blog/trust-the-new-workplace-currency/201309/ten-ways-cultivate-work-relationships-and-grow-trust.

6. R. Goffee and G. Jones (2006) *Why Should Anyone Be Led by You?* (Boston, MA: Harvard Business School Press).

7. C. M. Riordan (2014) "Three ways leaders can listen with more empathy." http://blogs.hbr.org/2014/01/three-ways-leaders-can-listen-with-more-empathy/.

8. K. Ferrazzi (2014) "Getting virtual teams right," *Harvard Business Review*, December. https://hbr.org/2014/12/getting-virtual-teams-right#signin.

9. A. Fraser (2012) "The 3rd space: How to show up with the right mindset every time." http://dradamfraser.com/about/services/keynote-speaking/the-3rd-space-managing-how-you-show-up.html#.VCDp2U0cSP8.

10. J. Maxwell (1993) *Developing the Leader Within You* (Nashville, TN: Thomas Nelson).
11. K. Patterson, J. Grenny, R. McMillan, and A. Switzler (2012) *Crucial Conversations: Tools for Talking When the Stakes are High*, 2nd ed. (London: McGraw-Hill).

8 Conversations for Making and Reviewing Decisions

1. P. Iyer (2013) "How to transform firms into networks," *The Australian*, (28 July).
2. T. Baker (2015) *The New Influencing Toolkit: Capabilities for Communicating with Influence* (London: Palgrave Macmillan).
3. ibid.
4. P. Senge (1999) *The Dance of Change* (A fifth discipline resource) (New York: Random House).
5. https://www.frames.gov/partner-sites/emissions-and-smoke/educational-resources/case-studies/the-atlanta-incident/the-after-action-review/.

10 Active Listening Can Make Other People Better Communicators Too

1. A. Ivey and J. Hinkle (1970) "The Transactional Classroom." Unpublished manuscript, University of Massachusetts. Cited in R. Bolton (1987) *People Skills: How to Assert Yourself, Listen to Others, and Resolve Conflicts* (East Roseville, Australia: Simon & Schuster).
2. B. T. Ferrari (2012) *Power Listening: Mastering the Most Critical Business Skill of All* (New York: Penguin).
3. D. Goleman (2013) "Curing the common cold of leadership: Poor listening," 2 May. https://www.linkedin.com/pulse/article/20130502140433-117825785-curing-the-common-cold-of-leadership-poor-listening (Accessed 4 Dec 2014).
4. R. G. Nichols and L. A. Stevens (1957) "Listening to people," *Harvard Business Review*, Sept–Oct.

11   Using Your Eyes (Part 1): Three Perceptual Positions

1. J. De Lozier and J. Grinder (1987) *Turtles All the Way Down: Prerequisites to Personal Genius* (Scotts Valley, CA: Grinder & Associates).
2. C. Feser, F. Mayol, and R. Srinivasan (2015) "Decoding leadership: What really matters," *McKinsey Quarterly,* January.
3. S. Covey (1990) *The 7 Habits of Highly Effective People: Powerful Lessons in Personal Change* (London: Prentice Hall).
4. http://www.inspirationalsolutions-nlp.co.uk/perceptual_positions.html.
5. http://www.nlpls.com/articles/perceptualPositions.php.

12   Using Your Eyes (Part 2): Watching and Being Watched

1. A. Mehrabian (1967) *Silent Messages: Implicit Communication of Emotions and Attitudes* (Belmont, CA: Wadsworth Publishing Company).
2. C. Kinsey Goman (2011) *The Silent Language of Leaders* (San Francisco, CA: Jossey-Bass)
3. A. O'Keefe (2011) *Hardwired Humans: Successful Leadership Using Human Instincts* (New South Wales: Roundtable Press).
4. D. Kahneman (2011) *Thinking, Fast and Slow* (London: Allen Lane).
5. A. Cuddy (2012) "Your body language shapes who you are," TEDGlobal (June). http://www.ted.com/talks/amy_cuddy_your_body_language_shapes_who_you_are.
6. E. Peper and I. Lin (2012) "Increase or decrease depression: How body postures influence your energy levels," *Biofeedback,* 40(3), Fall. http://biofeedbackhealth.files.wordpress.com/2011/01/a-published-increase-or-decrease-depression.pdf.
7. Kinsey Goman, *The Silent Language of Leaders.*

13   The Art of Inquiry in Conversations

1. M. Marquardt (2005) *Leading with Questions* (San Francisco, CA: Jossey-Bass).

2. ibid.

3. See http://en.wikipedia.org/wiki/Action_learning for a definition of action learning.

4. For more on the solution-focused approach, visit www.swork.com, an organization that promotes the solution-focused approach in management.

5. P. Senge (1990) *The Fifth Discipline* (New York: Doubleday).

6. I. Nonaka and N. Konno (1998) "The concept of *Ba:* Building a foundation for knowledge creation," *California Management Review,* 40(3), Spring.

14 Creating and Maintaining Safe, Open Feedback Channels

1. G. Hamel (2007) *The Future of Management* (Boston, MA: Harvard Business School Press).

2. C. E. Shannon (1948) "Mathematical Theory of Communication," *The Bell System Technical Journal,* 27, pp. 379–423, 623–56, (July, October)

3. J. Trueland (2014) "Make the pledge," *Nursing Standard*, 28(26), p. 3.

4. Hamel, *The Future of Management*.

5. ibid.

6. D. Goleman (2002) *The New Leaders* (London: Time Warner Books).

7. D. Rock (2008) "SCARF: A brain-based model for collaborating with and influencing others," *NeuroLeadership Journal*, Issue 1.

8. ibid.

9. A. Fraser (2012) "The separation of powers – approachable leaders," (19 July). http://www.dradamfraser.com/articles/editorial/separation-of-powers-approachable-leaders.html#.UqgG9tHxtMs.

10. A. Bryant (2011) "Google's quest to build a better boss," *New York Times*, 12 March. http://www.nytimes.com/2011/03/13/business/13hire.html?pagewanted=all.

11. D. Goleman and R. Boyatzis (2008) "Social intelligence and the biology of leadership," *Harvard Business Review*, September. https://hbr.org/2008/09/social-intelligence-and-the-biology-of-leadership/ib.

12. ibid.

Index

Printed and bound by CPI Group (UK) Ltd, Croydon, CR0 4YY